**Juliet Solomon**, who is a graduate in economics and is qualified to teach various aspects of social studies, has had a wide variety of jobs ranging from cleaning houses to running an adult education centre in South Yorkshire. She has written for several publications including *The Independent* and *Nursery World*, and has previously published two books, *Making Sense of Economics* (with Ross Chapman, Fontana, 1974) and *Holding the Reins*, a study of the nanny/employer situation in the late 20th century (Fontana, 1987).

Much of her time is now spent running Britain's first Junior Friends of the Earth group, working with schools and parents, and looking after her family. She is currently researching some of the lesser-known effects of television on children for her next book, *Programmed For Life*, which will also be published by Optima, in between digging an allotment and playing string quartets.

*O P T I M A*

# GREEN PARENTING

## JULIET SOLOMON

### ILLUSTRATED BY JENNIE SMITH

An OPTIMA book

© Juliet Solomon, 1990

First published in 1990 by
Macdonald Optima, a division of
Macdonald & Co. (Publishers) Ltd

A member of the Maxwell Macmillan Pergamon Publishing Corporation

British Library Cataloguing in Publication Data

Solomon, Juliet
    Green Parenting.
    1. Children. Home care
    I. Title
    649.1

    ISBN 0-356-18768-3

Macdonald & Co. (Publishers) Ltd
Orbit House
1 New Fetter Lane
London EC4A 1AR

Typeset in Century Schoolbook by
Leaper & Gard Ltd, Bristol

Printed and bound in Great Britain by
The Guernsey Press Co. Ltd, Guernsey, Channel Islands

# CONTENTS

# FOREWORD

Like so many others, I first became involved in what is now called 'the Green Movement' in the early '70s. At that time, I was resolutely childless, though already given to rather pompous utterances about the need to 'safeguard the future for our children and grandchildren by protecting the Earth'! Sixteen years on, with a lively and much-loved one-year-old daughter, those very vague and abstract concerns have become much more tangible and much more pressing. There *is* the future, after all, crawling around quite innocently in our midst!

Some of the anxiety pangs of a 'green parent' are already beginning to make themselves felt. Are we giving her the right kind of diet? Should we never have the television on when she happens to be with us in the sitting room? Just what is 'an environment-friendly nappy', let alone an 'ecologically-acceptable toy'? So I didn't hesitate at all when I was asked to do the foreword for *Green Parenting*, on the off-chance that I was going to pick up a few useful tips along the way.

In that, I have not been disappointed, as this is a book long on practical advice and intelligent ideas, and blissfully short on preaching. It is certainly not aimed at that tiny band of green paragons who make all the rest of us feel so inadequate, but acknowledges in a very sympathetic manner the genuine difficulties of bringing up children in a culture as transparently ungreen as ours.

Having been a teacher for ten years, I know only too well how powerful the process of 'cultural homogenisation' can be. Peer group pressures are bad enough for adults; for children, they can be deeply disturbing. There are few attractions at that age in being seen to be different — or indeed in one's parents being seen to be different!

But one of the more encouraging consequences of the current wave of interest in all things green is the massively increased level of awareness amongst young people. Peer group pressure works both ways, and if sufficient pressure can be exercised by committed and aware youngsters to encourage their colleagues — and parents! — to go a little green, then their world will indeed be a much safer place in the future.

Set against that, the power of the advertising industry and those vested interests whose fortunes depend on persuading people that 'you are what you own' is enormous. The sophisticated business of creating artificial needs in people starts at a very young age, and the insidious poison of advertising on children's television is doing as much to inculcate tragically corrupted attitudes in children as any other facet of our consumer-driven society.

It seems so utterly obvious that children should be brought up to care for the environment *in* a caring environment that one wonders why this still seems a distant ideal instead of a living reality for the vast majority of parents. The fact that so many children are obliged to grow up in impoverished and often poisoned environments powerfully reinforces vicious, interlocking circles of human and ecological degradation.

We have surely learned enough about the errors of our ways to insist that the potentiality of every child should be nurtured and nourished like a cherished seed in a rich and loamy soil. From that perspective, green parenting is not an optional extra; it is a precondition for creating any kind of compassionate and sustainable future for our children.

Jonathon Porritt
September 1989

# PREFACE

'Green parenting' is a new term. But although it may sound like a description of how Greenpeace or Friends of the Earth members might bring up their children, that is not what it means. Or not only that. It means a great deal more than the sum of its parts. For while this book concerns itself to a large extent with the practical and psychological implications of Green attitudes in our dealings with our children, it ends up being essentially about attitudes that promote human growth and the relationship of human growth to solutions to the global crisis. Although the practical solutions might be different with adults, anybody or anything could be Green parented.

In Chapter 1, some of the fundamental global problems and their roots are outlined. These problems are not isolated, but are effectively symptoms of an underlying lack of balance in the whole of the ecosystem, of which children are one, fairly large, part. Man's attitudes have been reflected in those of his actions which have caused, and are causing, damage to planet and people. While, therefore, much of this book is devoted to practical ideas, parts of it deal with issues that may at first sight appear unconnected to childrearing. I hope the relationship gradually becomes clear.

I have dealt in detail with attitudes and practicalities as they affect families. The nuts and bolts of Greener practices in daily homekeeping life are well documented elsewhere (see reading lists). I find some of these books helpful – I have not recommended any with which I am not familiar.

Much of what I have to say has been said before, more stylishly. Where it seemed to me that original statements still speak as clearly as when they were first written, I have quoted them unaltered. There is as little point in manufacturing new versions of durable, reusable words as there is of making new versions of reusable material goods. Recycling saves waste – and old, well-used words are often better than new ones.

An enormous number of people have contributed to the writing of this book, directly and indirectly, both adults and children. And it is the latter who often have clearer perceptions than adults but who are usually ignored by movements for change (the early women's liberation movement made this mistake). It would be a pity if the Green movement left them out. So I hope that this book, as well as helping adults, will help children to be accorded the respect and attention they deserve.

# ACKNOWLEDGMENTS

For direct contributions and amendments to the manuscript, Jill Williams, Cynthia Crosthwaite, Janet Halton, Howard Williams, Rachel Wheeler Robinson, Tanya Kenny and the Muswell Hill Mothers and Toddlers FoE, Rachel Williams, Brigid Cherry, Jonathon Porritt.

*Quaker Monthly*, and the newsletter of Colchester and Colchester monthly meeting where David Crouch's article on allotments first appeared.

For medical advice, Dr C. Hungerford BA, MB, BS.

For valuable time and ideas, Jean Liedloff, Mayer Hillman, Max Reid, David Fleming, Nicholas Robertson, Katharine Mackay, Katie Elliott, Robert Hare, Tina Detheridge, Frankie Weinberg, Ben Kerwood; several members of my local Friends of the Earth group and the junior group; members of Muswell Hill Meeting; Rosalind Richards and participants in the Music Camp, including my father, Dr J.D. Solomon; Richard Douthwaite; Faith Hall; and many, many others, notably my editor, Harriet Griffey, whose enthusiasm and support has been whole-hearted.

Finally my own family — Howard, a Green husband, and my children, Rachel and Michael who inspired the formation of our Juniors, and are a constant source of new inspirations and ideas, and perceptive detectors of adult inconsistencies!

The publishers would like to thank Jennie Smith for the illustrations.

To children, present and future,
and all who seek solutions.

There were on the planet where the little prince lived – as on all planets – good plants and bad plants. In consequence, there were good seeds from good plants, and bad seeds from bad plants. But seeds are invisible. They sleep deep in the heart of the earth's darkness, until someone among them is seized with the desire to awaken. Then this little seed will stretch itself and begin – timidly at first – to push a charming little sprig inoffensively upward toward the sun. If it is only a sprout of radish or the sprig of a rose-bush, one would let it grow wherever it might wish. But when it is a bad plant, one must destroy it as soon as possible, the very first instant that one recognises it.

Now there were some terrible seeds on the planet that was the home of the little prince; and these were the seeds of the baobab. A baobab is something you will never, never be able to get rid of if you attend to it too late. It spreads over the entire planet. It bores clear through it with its roots. And if the planet is too small, and the baobabs are too many, they split into pieces . . .

'It is a question of discipline', the little prince said to me later on. 'When you've finished your own toilet in the morning, then it is time to attend to the toilet of the planet, just so, with the greatest care. You must see to it that you pull up regularly all the baobabs, at the very first moment when they can be distinguished from the rose-bushes which they resemble so closely in their earliest youth. It is very tedious work', the little prince added, 'but very easy . . . Sometimes,' he added, 'there is no harm in putting off a piece of work until another day. But when it is a matter of baobabs, that always means a catastrophe.'

*The Little Prince*, Antoine de Saint-Exupéry

# 1.
# THE CONTEXT

The reader may wonder why a book about Green parenting should open with a lengthy quotation from *The Little Prince*, a novel written for 'grown-up children'. The reason is simple. St-Exupéry's novel is more than a delightful and moving story about a fantasy small boy who cares deeply about his planet: it is also a parable about the benefits of resistance to the fatuousness and destructiveness of many modern attitudes. The little prince's own outlook is based on care, love and attentiveness, and although new knowledge sometimes leads him into self-doubt, in the end he remains true to his values and preserves his happiness and serenity.

Can parents help their children to adopt such values? Should they? And, if so, how?

There are two major reasons for urgently and seriously questioning some of the attitudes and practices we are encouraged to adopt in modern industrial societies. The first of them is that, although many people are fairly happy, many others are affected by problems associated with stress, tension and dissatisfaction. Might there be other paths to higher levels of happiness than those which we usually follow? The second reason is possibly more powerful. If we do not rethink our attitudes and ways of life, we will greatly lessen the possibilities of a pleasant and sustainable lifestyle for future generations. Our children could have rotten adult lives.

At the time of writing, there is, almost daily, new evidence of man-made destruction and poisoning of people and planet. Seeds planted years ago in the interests of the short-term satisfaction of man are now becoming apparently uncontrollable plants. To take a few examples from the recent press:

- Tranquilliser pills in the benzodiazepines group are now reckoned (by mainstream scientists) to have caused as many problems as they have solved (*New Scientist*, 6 May 1989).
- The birth control pill may contain hormones which can trigger breast cancer (*Independent*, 5 May 1989).

- Intensive ranching of cattle for cheap meat is one of the reasons why the level of methane gas in the atmosphere is now increasing faster than the ecosystem can absorb it and recycle it (*Environment*, 10 November 1988).

This week, and next week, and the week after, we are almost bound to hear about more such problems.

Our children may already be suffering physically. Excellent health in children is surprisingly rare. It has been suggested that the increase in the number of children diagnosed as having chronic complaints such as allergies or asthma may be due to an increasingly toxic and stressful environment. In 20 years, today's children will, if environmental degradation continues at its present rate, have a great deal more to suffer from. They will also have to try to repair the damage to the environment, if it is not by that time irreparable.

Campaigning on children's behalf about issues that affect them is a start, but not enough. We also need to make a positive effort to equate our own Green attitudes with our attitudes to our children. Nurturing people or the planet are demanding and rewarding arts which, as will become clear, are closely related to each other and which, if well done, can result in personal and global wholeness and balance. But, as will also become clear, the odds are stacked against the skilled execution of these arts.

Essentially, the similarities between the problems of a disturbed (unbalanced) person and the problems arising from the disturbance of the balance of nature can be traced back to the same root – lack of care. (This might equally well be called lack of forethought, of husbandry, of disinterested love.) We can see the results of this all around us – on our neglected streets, in our polluted seas, in the prodigal manner in which we use many of our resources, and in the dissatisfied, grumbling and fearful lives of many adults and children. The lack of care which has led to this dreary and dangerous situation is one of the inevitable products of societies whose chief motives have for many decades been self-interest and private profit; societies which are involved in trying to make everybody pursue these same aims at the expense of other less materialistic goals.

Unfortunately, because we are all interdependent, even those who do not want to espouse the materialist cause are prevented from leading their chosen lifestyle. The world contains many unsung Greens who, without waving banners or joining movements, have looked after themselves and their planet with consistency and dedication. But their lives have been made progressively harder by the changes around them. They want appliances mended, and look for a mender, only to be told that replacement is the only possibility. They want to travel on buses, but the bus service is stopped and they are forced to buy cars. They want their children to learn gymnastics, but discover that gymnastics classes are devoted to badge-earning and competitions. Try as they might, they are dragged into the fast lane of living that they seek to avoid. They try to minimise the fast-lane effects as far as possible, but inevitably they have to compromise with mainstream values more than they would like.

However, there are cheerful signs on the horizon. The publicity accorded to global disasters, and what is likely to happen if we do not act fast to prevent them, is beginning to lead even those living in the fast-lane to begin to compromise in the other direction, with Green values. Many may not yet look like the typical Green (whatever that looks like), but they are at the beginning of the path. Being Green is in any case relative, for all of us who think of ourselves as in some way Green are on a kind of continuum in terms of the extent to which we feel able to change our lifestyles to compromise with some of our Green principles. At the far end are those who never have, and never will drive, a car, who live very simply on very little money, and whose daily activities have little in common with those of most of us. Further along the continuum are those who have given up one of their two cars, changed their washing-up liquid to an environmentally less harmful one, and have perhaps marginally simplified their lifestyles. Then there are those who have only recently become aware of those problems and have adapted all their cars to run on lead-free petrol. Finally, off the continuum, there are those who, despite what is happening to the world, do not consider it their business and continue as they always have.

The urgency of the global situation has caused many people to begin to rethink their attitudes and to modify their lifestyles and consumption patterns. However, for those who wish to make major changes, there are often considerable difficulties. One pig farmer decided that, although intensive pig farming had been less work and more profitable than the old-fashioned animal husbandry, he wanted the rewards of care. He had become very uneasy about modern methods; intuitively he had begun to feel it was wrong to jab his animals with hormones and antibiotics and keep them in rather crowded conditions, rather than look after them and give them a decent life. But before he could change his methods, he needed to find a sympathetic vet with the relevant skills and knowledge. And, he had to look for some considerable time and travel some distance before he could find one who knew anything about rearing pigs in harmony with nature.

For nurture, care and husbandry are not fashionable, and these arts are no longer given priority even in veterinary (or nursing, or teacher) training colleges. Instant, effortless, drug-aided solutions are taught in response to demand. Knowing which of these prepackaged solutions to use takes priority over knowing about humane and human solutions, which are considered too time consuming. This approach to the provision of solutions is increasingly common. And yet it is in direct conflict with one of the most fundamental human (and possibly animal) needs, which is personal attention.

The pressures of advertising and the promoting of painless and desirable lifestyles make it extremely difficult even to chart a course we feel might be more desirable, let alone to stay on it, without opting out of the mainstream of society altogether. Society sells us perfection, immediacy, painlessness, speed, achievement, excitement and self-aggrandisement (particularly financial) and it sells it to our children. What might be called the feminine aspects of life (see Chapter 14), which include patience, cooperation, responsiveness and stillness, are grossly undervalued by our culture. Sometimes even those of us who know them to be crucial to an enjoyable and fulfilling life are so besieged by the so-called 'masculine' alternatives that we find ourselves beginning to doubt the validity of the feminine principles. But without them we are out of balance.

In the cacophonous world in which we live it is hard to maintain a sense of harmony, of internal balance and balance with our surroundings. If we can guide our children towards this balance, giving them the internal strength to resolve the dissonances they will inevitably meet, encouraging their creative imaginations so that they can seek non-destructive solutions for themselves and others, and helping them to enjoy and appreciate the value of environmentally friendly and spiritually rewarding activities, we will have travelled a long way.

We owe it to our children to help them to learn attitudes which will put them in a position to solve their problems, because the world in which they are growing up is unlikely to be a benign one unless we act fast and help them to act. They themselves are increasingly aware of this. They see the results of the lack of care – the fact that nobody remembered to attend to the toilet of the planet because they were all too busy attending to their own toilet.

Rachel, who wrote the piece in the accompanying box, would probably not understand the complicated set of factors that have led to this situation, and the lack of respect for children, for their insights and for their place in the ecosystem that has led to their being overlooked. For the sake of her and her generation, we as parents need to understand and to be able to explain the issues and to try, against the will and efforts of the self-seeking society, to parent them Green.

---

Children are usually left out of big things. For example, if there was a petition against building on a wild piece of land, the adults would forget all about the children.

We need to take action to get new road crossings. Children now do not have as much freedom as would be nice. They cannot cross busy roads because of the dangerous traffic.

The streets are full of litter. They really shouldn't need cleaning if people didn't get away with dropping stuff. Litter spoils the environment. When cans are dropped, animals can get hurt on the sharp edges. It will all affect younger generations more because the adults will have grown old and frail before they could do anything about it.

Rachel, 9

---

## SOME MAJOR ENVIRONMENTAL PROBLEMS

Planet Earth is in a bad way. Man's lack of awareness of his relationship to the world around him has led to an unthinking and careless use of the world's resources, which in its turn has led to damage that threatens him and which will soon be beyond repair. Unfortunately, it is all too easy to ignore, for much of the damage currently being caused, unlike the damage caused by, for example, the first Industrial Revolution, is invisible to the naked eye. Argosies of mines and textile factories working around the clock to produce a continual stream of goods, and the accompanying thick clouds of smoke that hung over Blake's 'dark, satanic mills', could hardly be missed by even the most casual observer. Only a single breath or glance was needed to know that the side effects of this production could do nobody any good. But many of today's dangers are subtler, less visible, and easier to ignore. They are therefore far more insidious.

We have begun to act on the obvious and superficial problems. We can see the ugliness of industrial zones, and have developed design and landscaping methods to minimise their offensiveness. (But do we ever stop to wonder whether we need the goods they produce?) We have noticed that the streets are strewn with litter and know that something must be done; the 'Keep Britain Tidy' campaign has been working at this for decades. (But we don't often ask whether we need to generate so much litter, and furthermore we are allowing some of the principal generators of litter, fast-food chains, to whitewash their images by financially backing tidiness campaigns.)

Because we cannot see it, we have chosen to ignore scientists' warnings on the thinning of the ozone layer which absorbs damaging excesses of ultraviolet radiation from the sun, and which allows life on earth to flourish. It is now thinning out at an increasingly dangerous rate, which in turn allows cancer-inducing ultraviolet B radiation increasingly to get through the atmosphere. In time this will affect not only human life, but all other life forms. Much of the damage to the ozone layer appears to be caused by excessive use of chlorofluorocarbons (CFCs), a group of chemicals used as the propellant in aerosol cans, as well as in the 'blowing' of polystyrene packaging and in refrigerants (the liquids which circulate in refrigerators and freezers to carry heat away).

Damage to the ozone layer is only one part of the world's potentially biggest problem, the so-called greenhouse effect. Pollution of the atmosphere by greenhouse gases such as carbon dioxide and methane means that infra-red radiation (heat) cannot escape into the outer atmosphere. It appears that the earth's ecosystem will not be able to absorb the increasing production of greenhouse gases and that the temperature of the earth's surface is likely to rise, causing the melting of the polar icecaps, a rise in sea levels, and other climatic changes, including an increase in the destructiveness of hurricanes, crop losses and drought. The greenhouse effect is thought to be caused by the burning of fossil fuels, which produce carbon dioxide; the practice of intensive chemical farming and monocrop agriculture, which emits nitrous oxides; the intensive ranching of cattle, increasing the amount of methane in the atmosphere; indirectly by the use of chlorofluorocarbons (CFCs); and the destruction of the world's rain forests, both because the trees help to keep $CO_2$ levels in balance and because any burning of the timber itself contributes to the warming. And deforested land is then often used for intensive farming of one sort or another, which again adds to the greenhouse effect.

At ground level, the so-called Green revolution which has enabled farmers to produce enormously increased yields from each acre of land has left the soil (which contains living organisms and so needs nurturing) both full of chemicals, which drain into our water supplies, and devoid of the nutrition, which it needs for its long-term regeneration. In the 1930s huge areas in the United States became desert as a result of overgrazing and over-cultivation, and parts of Australia may be going the same way as well. The problem is not new.

The synthetic expansion of food production to provide cheap food (destined, it should be noted, for societies in which obesity is already a major cause of ill-health) means, furthermore, that it is no longer possible to know what is in the apples, the pound of beef or carton of milk bought for today's tea. The stimulation of animal growth and milk production with hormones is a common practice. Outbreaks of salmonella and listeria have brought the issues of food contamination to public notice but as with so many other long-term environmental problems, this contamination cannot be seen and often therefore is not taken very seriously.

These are only a few examples of the physical damage man is causing to his environment. However, the definition of damage needs to be widened to include the damage inflicted on people by other people. Apart from the fact that much of the world's population lives in abject poverty which could be alleviated by other nations if it were more visible, the affluence of western society is damaging the lives of a great many people who are neither starving nor at war. Indices of social disorder are rising, i.e. an increasing number of people are deemed to be unhappy and disaffected. Enormous quantities of psychotropic drugs are both prescribed and consumed without prescription. Crime, violence and alcoholism are rising, and loneliness appears to be a problem of millions. Humanity is in balance neither with itself nor with nature.

Cynics are in the habit of suggesting that this situation is endemic to man's condition and that such problems have existed since time began. But as far as we know the western world has never, until now, been in a situation where it was theoretically possible for everybody to be adequately fed, clothed and heated, and in which there should therefore be the possibility for people to expect to be reasonably happy. (Before the North American droughts of the last few years, enough food was produced globally for every human being to have between 2,500 and 3,000 calories a day each, which is above minimum nutritional levels.) Soil exhaustion due to intensive farming and population increases are changing the situation. However, a greater use of organic and biodynamic farming methods, coupled with more even food distribution and some population control would lessen the need for a massive increase in world food production levels and therefore the risk of more long-term damage to the planet and its population.

## WHY THE PROBLEM?

Various reasons have been suggested for the sadness of the current state of affairs. However, in the present context the reason that is clearest is man's greed, both innate and manufactured. It is not in the best interests of commercial business to allow anybody to feel contented. The man on a low income with deliberately few possessions is ascribed low status, although in Green terms he is the hero. Every effort is made to make him feel dissatisfied so that somebody can sell him something. The woman whose hair is mousy is persuaded by advertisers that she would look better if it were dyed blonde. I am persuaded to use henna to avoid what is socially considered premature greyness. Commuters on the Underground sit looking for hours at advertisements telling them they could have a better job with more pay if they used a certain employment bureau. Image after image suggests that we – the consumers – could do better materially, in status terms and emotionally ... if only. Countless images play on the fear that many of us have that we are not innately lovable, suggesting that we will be loved, if only – if only we used the right perfume, gave the right box of chocolates or bunch of prepackaged flowers, went to the 'right' places, served our husbands the right gravy, acquired the right level of suntan, or whatever. I shall be looking at some of these images later in the specialised context of parenting, but we are all being subjected to these powerful images much of the time.

In Aldous Huxley's *Brave New World* one of the slogans which children are taught to internalise from a very early age is 'Ending is Better than Mending'. The cult of the new and shiny is part of the pressure put on us all to teach us to despise that which is old and possibly shabby. This cult is not innate. The innocent infant often prefers the old, loved and grubby to the new and glossy. And the infant or small child, while she may be temporarily attracted to new faces and places, often carries on loving most those who are most familiar in her life, no matter what they look like or what treatment she receives from them. She often reacts the same way with objects too, rejecting the new Christmas present, after an initial flirtation, in favour of the old toy she knows and has loved, which has meaning for her because she has loved it (see the end of Chapter 14).

Much of *Brave New World*, while it may have seemed fantastic at the time when it was written, is with us now. The one factor which Huxley seems not to have anticipated was the effect that our levels of consumption would have on global and atmospheric resources. (However, since the culture of beauty and youth he portrayed caused people to die at 60, his population was controlled.) Huxley's world had got beyond the need for aggressive selling and marketing techniques. People no longer had to be persuaded; being battery-bred, they did what they were programmed to do. We have not yet reached that stage. Our producers are still desperately seeking to create markets for new products, many of which are at best spurious and at worst damaging, physically, emotionally and spiritually. What good can it do anyone to buy a gun which you can safely fire at your television set? The idea is grotesque, but people have been persuaded to buy them. What can a video on breastfeeding tell you that you could not easily find out for free from a breast-feeding mother? Another grotesque idea, unless it's disguised pornography. What is the point of buying a new car which will go at 200 kilometres per hour when your old car works and the speed limit is 120 kph?

Producers continue to saturate the adult market; they do very well with youth; they have created a new market for 'maturer people' (older people); and before that they launched a fierce invasion into the world of children and the parents of young children. Parents don't want to displease their children, so advertising aimed directly at the children is very effective because the child makes the parents' lives miserable until they buy what he thinks he wants. But much of the advertising (and when I refer to advertising I mean not only obvious advertising but advertising disguised as news) is aimed directly at parents and parents-to-be.

## PARENTS UNDER ATTACK

The role of parents, and the importance of everything they do for their children, has quite rightly been elevated from the lowly status it once had to that of artist and technician. But during this process a childcare industry has grown up, composed not only of those who want to sell their products but also of those who are selling their expertise. This help is necessary and desirable in a society short of personal links, where help is hard to come by. But it does have the effect of turning childcare into yet another set of techniques, whose secrets are known by experts, rather than encouraging its consumers to think out their own purposes in life and to try and relate their own childcare to these purposes and to their own feelings. Dr Spock points this out in *Baby and Child Care*, saying that unless parents have goals, childcare handbooks cannot ultimately be very useful. James Dobson, the American childcare writer, goes one step further and relates his methods directly to his stated Christian beliefs. There is no ideal form of childcare. There will be different means to different ends.

This book is concerned with parenting with Green goals. What these are precisely will vary from one person to the next. But if they are borne in mind, it is easier to parent in a way which will do less planetary damage and help to solve the problem.

## THE TRAP OF ECONOMICS

Many years ago the American economist J.K. Galbraith suggested that we were moving into an era in which increased private affluence would be matched with increased public squalor. In *The Affluent Society* he analysed the economics that have led to this situation. Classical economics, as applied to the western world, was the product of a harsh world of mass poverty, and its rules and institutions were established to try and give everybody a decent living in a situation where goods were scarce. Nobody wondered what would happen when goods were no longer scarce, except the producers of goods. They were faced with a buying public which had begun to satisfy its basic demands for food, shelter, warmth and a few extras. There was, in reality, no longer a strong case for the urgency of production. We could have started to take other goals more seriously – justice, the quality of life, altruism, to quote a few examples – had we so desired. Instead, producers set out on the quite unjustifiable road of producing 'wants'; unjustifiable, because it distorted the notion of wants and distracted men from other goals. The emphasis at the end of the quote in the box is mine; it gives an important perspective on our children, and what we expose them to. The conventional approach is that, in general, more of anything is better than less of it. Most things, anyway. But even in the 1960s Galbraith was not the only economist to point out that this was not necessarily the case.

Were it so that a man on arising each morning was assailed by demons which instilled in him a passion sometimes for silk shirts, sometimes for kitchenware, sometimes for chamber pots, and sometimes for orange squash, there would be every reason to applaud the effort to find the goods, however odd, that quenched his flame. But should it be that his passion was the result of his first having cultivated the demons, and should it also be that his effort to allay it stirred the demons to ever greater and greater effort, there would be question as to how rational was his solution. *Unless restrained by conventional attitudes, he might wonder if the solution lay with more goods or fewer demons.*

J.K. Galbraith, *The Affluent Society*

Conventional economics is too limited to solve our present problems. One of its main preoccupations, and justifications for its existence, has been its attempts to try to assess the relative costs and benefits of various actions. These are normally evaluated in money terms. But this kind of evaluation takes no account of costs that may be incurred in the very long term, such as medical treatment of workers in chemicals factories, costs of grassing over slag heaps, costs of removing harmful pollutants that have drained from fields into the water supply. Nor does it take into account costs which cannot be measured in monetary terms, such as the stress of living beside an airport, the spoliation of the landscape by the erection of a hideous building next to a beauty spot, the destruction of human relationships through work-related tensions, the destruction of human dignity and spirit through mind and soul-destroying jobs, the loss of hearing (however minor) incurred by many as a result of a noisy environment, the loss of sleep caused by whole streets being woken night after night by burglar alarms on cars – and many, many others. Because these cannot be measured in money terms, economists simply ignore their existence.

More of anything, however desirable, is likely to produce at least a bit more of something undesirable, even if great care is taken. There are always unknown factors, although the effect of these can be considerably reduced if there is less haste and more research before projects are undertaken. But any action involves some risk. This is not an argument for not acting, but it is an argument against actions dependent on short-term economic or scientific measurement. Many actions would have been better not taken. The production of goods with built-in obsolescence springs to mind. The wholesale use of plastics would be another example, as would the wholesale use of DDT. All these actions were justified in terms of short-term economic benefits.

Unfortunately, the assumption that more is better than less has been made a dominant assumption – even though over-eating, excessive speed, excessive alcohol and overwork are known killers of people, and excessive production is known to be damaging the ecosystem. There is, however, a growing minority of people (including a few economists) who dispute this assumption and are concerned to point out that not only have we reached the point of production where continued expansion may bring more long-term costs than it will benefits, but that living less extravagantly and more thoughtfully might provide a higher level of human happiness than many people currently experience. And once the conventional assumption is seen to be false, many other associated assumptions have also to be disputed. This could have a considerable effect on our children's lives, so we must consider what new economics might mean for them.

## THE PLACE OF WORK IN A GREEN SOCIETY

Those defending the creation of more consumer wants have often pointed out that less consumption means less employment. Which it undoubtedly does, if employment is interpreted as a means of making money. But if the acquisition of material wealth were not the primary goal, people would be able to cope with less paid employment, provided they had an adequate standard of living and provided also they were not made to feel guilty if they were neither earning money nor consuming. If they could still remember how to 'play' using their own resources, as adults, some people would be blissfully happy. I met a delightful man at a skip one day who was salvaging a bookcase, who told me that he had been made redundant five years previously (he was in his late 40s) and that he had never enjoyed himself as much as he did now. He went fishing, read, worked for voluntary agencies, on an income which he said was low enough to free him from all his previous pressures. He liked what he was doing as he did it. If the emphasis on what was worthwhile in life were placed less on product and more on process, many people could find worthwhile occupation. To start with, clearing up the mess we have made of our world and its people could keep millions of people occupied for many years. This kind of work needs patience and care, however, and it would be only possible for its personal and social rewards to be keenly felt if society at large placed more value on care.

It is a sad fact that although the maintenance of the paid work ethic and the status it confers is necessary in our consumer-oriented society, work itself is often not much enjoyed. Many people work only for their pay packet, which is hardly surprising given the nature of much of the work. And even if somebody did happen to enjoy filling supermarket shelves from nine at night until seven in the morning, they would find it socially unacceptable to say so (partly because, if the work-loving mentality could be cultivated, it would contain the real danger that people's goodwill could be exploited, as it is in some of the 'caring' professions).

However, it is not just the paid work that is regarded as a chore. The number of labour-saving devices for the home to be found on the market suggests that the manufacturers would like consumers to feel that any labour is to be avoided. A cake, for example, can be satisfactorily and enjoyably mixed using a bowl and a wooden spoon; indeed, much of the joy in baking a cake is being in touch with the texture and the materials used. And clearly, if somebody is producing cakes because he has to, rather than because he wants to, it makes sense to save labour. But the makers of the machines produced to do the mixing are elevating the message that cake-making is a chore above the message that the process of cake-making can be literally a labour of love.

One day Mr Jones was spotted by a neighbour cutting his lawn with a pair of dressmaking scissors. His neighbours offered to lend him a lawnmower, but it turned out that he already had one. He was cutting the lawn with scissors because, rather than do it very quickly with a noisy machine and then sit around doing nothing, he wanted to get on quietly with doing something outdoors, paying attention to detail, mothering the grass (and the daisies, which he was able to cut round) in a way which was normally precluded by lack of time. He found it creative and therapeutic – he was happy doing it. The neighbours found this hard to understand, for we are conditioned to use a machine, wherever possible, whatever the aims of our activity. It is assumed that activity is about the achievement of product and not the enjoyment of process. Mr Jones was serving his own ends, using the appropriate technology, rather than allowing the machine to dictate what he should do. He was meeting his own needs, at no cost to anybody else. Most work does not perform this function for workers. Work is now intimately linked to technological performance and to servicing the goals of production. We end up being at the service of our machines, and this is why the Greens have placed so much importance on finding appropriate technologies.

APPROPRIATE TECHNOLOGIES

The terms low, intermediate and high technology appear a great deal in Green writings, and it is often assumed that the Green path is anti-technology, which it is not. However, the Green approach, which owes a great deal to the writings of Fritz Schumacher and James Robertson, among others, does differ radically from the conventional approach. The appropriate use of technology is not only environmentally desirable, but can contribute to psychological wellbeing in both adults and children.

All technology is an extension of human capacity. A knife

helps our hands and teeth at mealtimes. A box of matches enables us to create fire without arduous toil. A bicycle, or a motor car, enables us to travel faster than our legs can carry us, although the same journeys would theoretically be possible on foot. Some technology makes the impossible possible – a boat enables journeys to be undertaken which are beyond the capacity of a swimming human, and a computer can perform calculations in a few minutes which might take an individual a lifetime.

Faults in our technological extensions often feel similar to malfunctionings of our own systems; the feeling of trying to drive a failing car up a steep hill is akin to that of walking with a bad leg, and losing the information from a computer disc can feel like losing one's memory. At a simpler level, the expiry of a torch battery at night is like losing one's sight. Those who have never used cars become highly proficient at travelling without them; those who live in oral cultures often remember what we might need to write down; those who have no torches are said to develop good night vision. So although every technological advance brings an extension to our human faculties, something else simultaneously contracts. This can be described as a 'cost', although it is often a price worth paying.

Technological advance brings costs to society, social costs, as well as to the individual. Old torch batteries are environmentally polluting. Universal ownership of motor cars brings increased mobility only as long as the roads are not too clogged up; and the other social costs of the motor car include air pollution, country-side carved up for roads, towns torn apart and made dangerous, increased hazards for children and old people, noise, and many others.

The motor car can be described as a high-tech solution to the travel problem, although clearly it is not as high-tech as an aeroplane or rocket. The zero-tech solution is legs. The inter-mediate technology solution (intermediate technology is a favourite of the Greens) is a bicycle, which speeds up the indi-vidual's travel substantially while having few, if any, harmful side effects, and having positive benefits on the individual's health and sense of wellbeing. For city journeys of about five miles the bicycle is in many respects the most efficient and the 'best' solution.

Schumacher, in *Small is Beautiful*, points out that:

the type of work which modern technology is most successful in reducing or even eliminating is skilful, productive work of human hands, in touch with real materials of one kind or another ... A great part of the modern neurosis may be due to this very fact; for the human being, defined by Thomas Aquinas as a being with brains and hands, enjoys nothing more than to be actively, usefully, productively engaged with both his hands and his brains.

But Schumacher's preoccupations are not those of the makers of modern technology. We have long since stopped making a priority of the idea that the economy, and therefore work, should be oriented towards making each individual feel good in himself. High-technology solutions provide more goods faster, and are therefore assumed better than other solutions, whatever the nature of the work involved or the nature of the product. The best possible solution to the Green is not necessarily the one which provides maximum output at minimum speed and minimum monetary cost. The ideal technology would be that which makes the maximum contribution to the aims stated on pages 20–21. Frequently the answers lie in the intermediate technology solutions. On a global level, for example, the answer to food production would be biodynamic or organic farming, rather than intensive cultivation. More dignified employment is provided at less cost to the planet. The answer to the energy problem would be conservation (intermediate/low/high technology) and the use of natural energy sources, not the high-tech nuclear power solution which has an unknown number of social costs.

The point can be made with a local rather than a global example. Jack has a concrete-set path in his garden which is an eyesore and which he therefore wants to remove. He can try and get it up using brute force, which might prove impossible. He can do it manually, using well-designed picks and shovels and his own energy. Or he can hire a pneumatic drill and, with a lot of noise and air pollution and the chance of some unintentional damage, break it up at high speed. What should he do?

He has a family, and they enjoy doing things together. Furthermore, they all like to contribute to the garden. They could not help if he were to use the drill. So on a sunny Sunday he and all the family get down to work with picks, shovels, hands and a wheelbarrow. At the end of the day they are well exercised and content. They have spent a productive afternoon together in the sun, each working at his own speed and capacity, and taking time off to play. Since no tool has to be returned to a tool-hire firm, there is no hurry. The job gets done. There is a sense of family teamwork and personal satisfaction, and the old slabs are standing against the wall waiting to be re-used.

Jack could have worked a few hours overtime in his office to pay for the drill – and then paid for the family to do something with their leisure. And his solution might not be judged the most 'efficient'. But it was the best course of action. But to know that it was the best demands that we forget that the best would usually be taken as meaning the quickest, most 'convenient' option. Yet if we watch children, and ask ourselves whether they get more joy from high or intermediate tech, roller skating may well beat the rides of the leisure park.

Intermediate technology solutions take into account not just the product but also the human and environmental costs and benefits of the process. Clearly, high technology is often useful, and there will always be occasions when we buy something, or do something only because it is instrumental in furthering some other purpose. But we need to remember that ignoring processes and their side-effects has done considerable harm. However, to think about process for much of our time demands a shift of perspective and an ability to concentrate, which is difficult to achieve in a world so full of variety, novelty and jobs which somebody has persuaded us need to be done, whether we like them or not.

## RIGHTS AND RESPONSIBILITIES

Consideration of the side-effects of our behaviour, of our lives, is not something that comes naturally in a world more devoted to the individual's rights. Most of the current demands for rights arose out of perceived injustices, but they now go far beyond the redress of injustice. We want consumer rights, rights to education, health rights, parking rights, and many others. However, such rights are only one side of a coin. On the other side there is the neglected notion of responsibility. If we have a right to cheap food, do we also have a right to expect that its quality shall be as high as that of more expensive food? If so, who should be responsible for monitoring its quality? Should we hold ourselves responsible for the damage to the rainforests when we eat beefburgers? If we have a right to housing, should we not take the responsibility for maintaining its fabric? If we have a right to drive motor cars, do we not have a responsibility to do something about their deleterious side-effects? All our actions lead to consequences which may or may not be desirable. An over-emphasis on personal 'freedom' can lead to consequences being ignored, or, put another way, responsibilities being overlooked. One man's present freedom may imply the present or future suffering of others. Even childcare writers who consider the child's freedom of paramount importance have modified their thinking, suggesting that children might benefit more from a clear set of values and the responsibilities that these imply.

In a morally pluralistic society, the onus is on individual families to help children to develop their values. Parents provide the environment which provides the child with a basis for her own judgements, and the confidence with which to act on them. This can be difficult for those who not only have no experience of children but who also have themselves been reared in a climate in which the rejection of existing social and moral values has had priority over the development of alternatives, thus allowing materialistic values to prevail. So many parents are parenting in a vacuum that it is easy for the salesmen of child-care products and childcare advice to step in with goods and advice which may prove undesirable and should certainly be unnecessary. The 'perfect parenting' message is sold as though it is morally neutral, which psychology cannot be. It is accompanied by all kinds of material accoutrements, and parents often find there is no time to give them serious consideration – they do what seems easiest at the time. Because of the pace of life and lack of time, many parents say that they have really only stopped to think about values after their children were born, and have frequently ended up *reacting* to situations rather than having any consistent criteria and acting purposefully. The urgency of the global situation and the absolute need to think should concentrate minds enormously.

The values which underlie the contents of this book are, put very simply:

- The steady-state economy, i.e. an economic system in which sustainability takes priority over economic growth.
- The use of technologies which serve human and personal goals rather than serving the goal of the production of

maximum output at minimum monetary cost.

- Decentralisation – the return of greater control to the individual, family and local community, and away from large, centralised organisations whose goals may not relate to local needs.
- A sustainable balance between humans and the rest of nature.
- Reverence for life on earth.

> I think that more of our children would grow up happier and more stable if they were acquiring a conviction, all through childhood, that the most important and the most fulfilling thing that human beings can do is to serve humanity in some fashion and to live by their ideals.
>
> Dr Spock, *Baby and Child Care*

We have considered several of these principles in a general way. For humanity to move forward, or even to survive, we do not have to turn the clock back, but we have got to progress down a different path to our present one. As parents, whatever the odds against us, we have to try to bring up children who are competent and internally happy, free from the treadmill of a compulsive drive for acquisition, over-excitement and selfishness. Instead they will have energy, zest for life and the confidence (self-esteem) which will help them to restore the planet and at least some of its occupants to a state of wellbeing. Sometimes it may seem like an uphill struggle. It would be easy to give in to the temptation to buy another toy to keep Johnny amused, or to stick him in front of the video with a polystyrene carton of junk food. Sometimes we're bound to find ourselves doing this. But it is in order to be better able to resist making this way of life a habit that we require more confidence in our own ideas than we have ever needed.

## FURTHER READING

*Small is Beautiful,* E.F. Schumacher, Abacus, London, 1974. A study of economics as if people mattered. This is a classic text and has spawned many ideas.

*The Sane Alternative – Signposts to a Self-Fulfilling Future,* James Robertson, 1978. A vision of a saner future and how it might be achieved.

*Seeing Green,* Jonathon Porritt, Basil Blackwell, Oxford, 1984. A compelling read – an examination of society as it now is and why it needs to be Greened. Very personal, as you can see the author's own journey into Greenness. Reads very easily, like an after-dinner conversation with a friend.

*The Little Prince,* Antoine de Saint-Exupéry, Puffin, London, 1962. Children see more than we do.

*Brave New World,* Aldous Huxley, Penguin, London, 1955. A classic – an imaginative picture of a dreary dehumanised future which we have just about reached. Very inspiring, if not a 'great' novel. Short and easy to read.

*The Affluent Society,* J.K. Galbraith, Penguin, London, 1987. A visionary classic.

*The Future of Work,* Charles Handy, Basil Blackwell, Oxford, 1984. Looks at possible scenarios.

For information on the present state of the world, the *State of the World 1989,* Worldwatch Institute, W.W. Norton, 37 Great Russell Street, London WC1B 3NU, gives a useful picture. It is updated annually.

# 2.
# FROM CONCEPTION TO 15 MONTHS

## PREGNANCY AND BIRTH

It was Saturday afternoon, and the train was returning from the West End of London. A worried-looking heavily pregnant woman and her male escort were clutching three massive Mothercare bags. Exhausted, he tried to look interested as she looked through them and said 'Do you think we've got everything we need?'

'I don't know,' he said, 'but it's cost a lot more than I thought it would.' They relapsed into gloomy silence.

A few minutes later she spoke. 'I hadn't realised,' she said.

'What?' he replied.

'Just how much we were going to need.'

Two stops later, quietly and sadly, they crawled off the train. Their first baby, even before being born, was already a financial burden. The afternoon that they could have spent enjoying themselves had been spent staggering up to the West End for a reluctant bout of consumerism.

For all this is now part of the conventional preparation for birth. The concept of what the baby and pregnant mother need has been defined by those who have something to sell. One catalogue has two whole pages devoted to toiletries for the pregnant woman. She doesn't know what is happening to her, but is informed by the catalogue that 'during pregnancy the many changes which occur in your body will be reflected by your skin. Thus we have developed ... a new luxury range of body care products, etc., etc. And the result? Beautiful, softer, clearer skin.' Can a cream really be formulated which 'specially tones hips and thighs'? Such a statement is a typical part of the marketing strategy which plays on the pregnant woman's fear of losing her youth and beauty.

Almost all maternity preparations are irrelevant, including a lot of maternity clothes, until the last few months of pregnancy. However we all need to feel we have influence on our situation, and one of the major problems of being pregnant is that, apart from eating sensibly and having regular checks, there is no way in which the pregnant woman can control what is happening to her. All she can do about it is to react to what her body tells her. Unless she gets very large very fast, there is no need for a great many special clothes; it is astonishing what a piece of elastic will do if fixed between button and buttonhole on the waistband of a skirt or trousers, which can be worn with a loose smock or shirt (perhaps one of her husband's shirts, with the bottom turned up, and dyed). She's certainly going to need a bigger bra, but again a piece of elastic at the back of an ordinary one does for quite a long time. It's probably worth buying one nursing bra in late pregnancy that will do after the baby is born (unless you can find a friend who will lend you one) – but only one, because it's not easy to predict what size you will need. It's actually perfectly possible to nurse from an ordinary old stretchy bra, and a lot easier than fiddling around with hooks and eyes.

The ideal solution is to do without. There are medical reasons why this is the case. A major cause of feeding failure is flattened or inverted nipples, which may be caused by the wearing of a badly fitting bra. After birth, the freedom helps nipples to breathe, and lowers the possibility of infection. Many anti-leak devices put inside bras are plastic, and raise the possibility of breast infection. To be free to go without, you need to switch off from catalogue images of young mothers. Breastfeeding and glamour just don't really go together. If you can persuade yourself to wear old clothes and not mind the odd leak at those times of the day when your public appearance is unimportant, you will save yourself a lot of trouble, and you can still switch on the glamour if and when it is needed.

During the last few months of pregnancy, certainly, the mother-to-be can feel a bit dreary, wearing the same old clothes. It's useful to be able to borrow from somebody who's recently delivered, or to team up with equally pregnant people and pass clothes around, just for a change. (This is made simpler if you belong to a group such as the National Childbirth Trust, NCT, where you will meet several other people at the same stage of pregnancy.) If you can acquire one really nice outfit that makes you feel good, this can help at the stage when you might be a bit fed up with feeling dowdy.

A great deal has been written about how important it is for the pregnant woman to be positive about her own pregnancy, and how to listen to her body. But she can not only feel demeaned by the images of good cheer and glamour provided by the culture; she can also feel unimportant when faced by some hospitals, whose routines can be reminiscent of a production line. Women can sit for hours waiting for routine tests and measurements, often never seeing the consultant who is nominally in charge of them and often not being told why particular tests are necessary. Various groups, notably the NCT, have inspired many hospitals to improve the situation, but the way hospitals have to work and the scale on which they must operate means that they are necessarily depersonalised.

Giving birth is a very ancient affair. At one time it used to be a rather dangerous business, but the intermediate technology involved in improved health, sanitation and antenatal care has removed most of the dangers. However, hospitals and hospital doctors are oriented towards high technology, and have managed to convince the public and themselves that the safest – and therefore the best – place to give birth is in hospital. Although there are clear instances in which hospital technology saves lives and helps in other ways, this technology is only required in a very few cases and its presence can often impede a relaxed delivery. But the more it is used, the more indispensable it seems to become.

Despite admirable attempts to promote home births, the supply of trained personnel available to attend at home deliveries is diminishing. Home births emphasise control by people and not technology. At a home birth a father, in particular, has a function which is simply not available in hospital; it is at a home birth that he has one of the best chances in his life to exercise fully his nurturing skills.

Once upon a time, safe home delivery was common. It still is in Holland, where flying squads are equipped to deal with emergencies. Not only is this good for family relationships and a boost to people's self-esteem, but it is a far more efficient use of resources than hospital delivery. And the care is of high quality. The same, known people see the mother through most of her labour, unlike in hospital where several faces may be present at delivery which have never previously been seen by any member of the family – while these people undoubtedly discharge their duties more than adequately, their lack of personal involvement means that they cannot be as genuinely concerned in the process as those known more intimately.

The system whereby your own doctor and a known midwife deliver you in hospital and you go home after a few hours – a so-called domino (domiciliary, in and out) delivery – may be the best of both worlds, and has a lot to recommend it. It is personal, and it puts high technology in its appropriate place in human activity; it is available if needed, but is not central to the midwife's thinking. However, the booklet given out by the Health Education Authority to every expectant mother devotes a page and a half to hospital deliveries, enumerating all of their advantages and none of their disadvantages, and suggesting questions you might like to ask about them. GP unit deliveries, domino deliveries and home deliveries get only three-quarters of a page between them – and not one single advantage is given for a home birth.

A child's first impressions of the world can, we are told, be very important. And if he can be born into an atmosphere of calm, surrounded by people who can relate to each other, rather than by machines and the inevitable disturbances of a hospital, he is then a part of the family's continuum. Clearly the child born in hospital is not irreparably damaged at birth, but the child born at home has started a new life within that house. He will also have brought a lot of extra work which, although it may seem tedious at the time, is life-enhancing for those who have to do it.

Once the baby is born, the hospitalised mother is often deluged with gifts and samples of babycare products (it used to come in one bag, and be known as the 'Bounty bag'). This is the beginning of the insidious process of making mothers feel that there are certain things that must be bought for the baby, a process that can have a dramatically debilitating effect. On the ward at my first birth one girl was in deep distress because she had no cot at home for her baby and thought she had better leave the baby in hospital overnight while she went out and bought all the kit. She was very relieved when told the baby could go on sleeping with her, as it had in the hospital, or that she could put him to sleep in a drawer or cardboard box at her mother's. But she would probably not have been put in this distressed situation had it not been for the messages she had been getting from the books and magazines in the hospital. (It didn't help watching all the other mothers leaving with elaborately kitted out babies, positively sparkling with shiny newness.)

## REJECTING THE CULT OF STERILITY

The sparkle, the shine, the sterility, need to be part of the hospital mentality. Infections can easily spread in hospital. But this mentality is not appropriate or necessary at home. However, the need for pristine whiteness has been made a cultural obsession.

Years of advertising of the virginal but aggressive whiteness produced by Brand X detergent, and years of glossily clean tables and desks in television serials, have conditioned both our outer and our inner eye into a mentality which finds it difficult to tolerate the imperfections implied by anything that could pass as grubbiness. Our inner fear of being slightly stained has been enormously exacerbated by the sellers of whitening goods. These include not only the washing powders, fabric conditioners, sterilants of one sort or another, and all the rest of the environmentally damaging packets and sprays with which we are told to fill our kitchen cupboards, but also the energy-consuming hardware – washing machines, tumble driers, sterilisers, dishwashers, and all the accompanying accessories, the so-called white goods. Some of them are quite useful, but they have personal as well as environmental disadvantages.

> My mother's old washing machine has two programmes; Hot and Not Very. Mine has 21 and I don't have 21 things to wash. My mother has one of those clothes driers you hoist up to the ceiling. Her washing is dry in an hour, free. My brand-new dryer runs for 180 minutes, gobbles up money and still leaves the T-shirts soggy ... Day by day I grow more uneasily sure that the much-vaunted technological miracles of our apparently computerised, privatised, post-modernised society are really a form of mass hypnosis practised upon us by a few Wizards of Oz.
>
> Jill Tweedie, *Independent*, 3 April 1989

Nobody would advocate a return to scrubbing clothes on a washboard as a way of life. But when it was a way of life, less washing 'needed' doing. Even as recently as the 1950s, the idea of a washday meant something. Although it took a long time it was *the* day when the washing was done, and the rest of the week was free of it. Now, because the machine is in the corner, every day can be washing day. This quite unnecessarily and extraordinarily time-and-energy-wasting habit is reinforced in the infant-rearing literature by an image of cleanliness which cannot be contemplated unless everything is washed every day.

This includes the baby, and his daily bath. Bathing the baby is a technique taught in hospitals. It is often fairly daunting to the new parent, as among other gems of advice given in books is a section on how to react if the baby is frightened. Which might just make one ask, 'Why on earth do it at all?'

Some babies like baths. But judging from the number of instructions given to make sure baby is happy, an awful lot don't. And the whole performance can actually be scrapped. A flannel and some warm water will get the baby perfectly clean, and if she does appear to need the occasional real soak, she'll probably enjoy getting into the bath with Mum or Dad. They'll enjoy it as well, and it'll save water.

The ritualised bath has generated a whole host of accessories – baby bath towels (why? a towel is a towel); things to put in the water, special soaps, bubbles, bath-mats. All the cosmetics are supposedly prepared 'for baby's delicate skin', but does he need a preparation containing formaldehyde in his bath? At least one of the best known bath products contains this powerful allergen, which also dries out his skin. It does of course, provide a good reason to buy the after-bath cream made by the same manufacturer. The baby's skin is delicate. Since the ingredients of most of these products are unstated, the best way to protect him from allergies or reactions is to avoid them altogether. This saves money, too.

For every individual there is a balance to be struck between too much and too little washing or bathing. Mother Nature has provided our skin with protective natural oils; if too much of the oil is washed out, it may need artificial replacement. Furthermore, the action of sunlight on the skin produces vitamin D, important in the development of strong bones. The nutritionist Adelle Davis suggests that soap and too frequent bathing may wash some of this valuable vitamin straight down the drain.

The whole palaver, if not an enjoyable experience for babies, can be dispensed with. If they like it, bung them in the bath, forgetting about cotton-wool balls, wet-wipes and the rest of it.

All you need is a flannel or a sponge or two. Not even soap is necessary.

The customary change of clothing (or twice or thrice-daily change) is also not essential. As adults we sweat a great deal, so many adults find that a daily change, at least of underwear, is more comfortable than no change. But babies do not sweat in the same way. They are rather clean. If they should happen to defaecate in a way that messes up their clothes or sheets, or they throw up all over their clothes, then clearly a change would be desirable. (The smell, incidentally, can quickly be got rid of with bicarbonate of soda sprinkled on it.) Otherwise, much of the dirt on their clothes is likely to be whatever has been caused by the hands of adults holding the child, and is pretty harmless. Babies don't really need changing at night, either, although some people feel that doing this after they are a few weeks old accustoms them to a day/night routine. Later on during the first year, when they are crawling around, their clothes really do begin to get dirty (although not from indoor crawling). And the year after that they will be filthy. So it is worth getting into the habit of doing the minimum amount of washing from the word go.

The exception is nappies, which do need changing, and washing if you use terry nappies. The habitual use of disposable nappies is not really justifiable in Green terms, although they are now taken for granted. In fact, the childcare literature has now moved the nappy debate away from the disposables v. terries argument, and has started to compare brands of disposables. This is unforgivable in a world which needs its trees, used for making disposables, and does not need the excess plastic to dispose of. Further, in order to up their sales, the disposable nappy manufacturers are attempting to create another market, by making differently styled girls' and boys' disposable nappies.

Terries can be bought as seconds or even secondhand, if the initial expense seems too much, and if they're dropped in a bucket of water with tea tree oil or ordinary washing soda in it to soak, and rinsed through, they only need a hot wash to keep them clean enough particularly if they are dried in the sun. There is a problem though for a Green parent; ecological detergents will not get them as white as chemicals. And although it may sound feeble, it's not easy to look at one's pile of greying nappies when other people's dazzle. We can take a tip from the disposable manufacturers here. They have discovered that the kinds of bleaches used to produce their magical whiteness may be bad for the baby's skin and are certainly environmentally damaging – so they are changing their colour. 'Now from —— comes a creamy coloured nappy that really stands out from the rest' the advertisement reads; the baby in the picture (although still as fair-haired as most of the images of children in the magazine) is playing, not with white feathers as he would have done a year previously, but with beige ones. If childcare can follow this manufacturer (without actually encouraging the use of his largely superfluous product) down the road to creaminess – perhaps bravely calling it beige or grey – an awful lot of unnecessary work will be saved both by us and our children, since they won't have whiteness engraved upon their sub-conscious. and the planet will be saved from bleaches, deter-gents, and excessive use of very hot water.

It is possible, for those who are brave enough, to go one stage further and leave the baby's nappy off completely for as much of the time as possible. They don't spend all day weeing, and the odd spill can easily be mopped up and doesn't stain. And it is usually possible to tell when they are about to defaecate, and hold them over a cloth or the loo. They have a good deal more freedom like this, and you may find you are only using about two nappies a day. And they don't get nappy rash. A pair of ordinary cotton knickers does quite well, or nothing at all. And it makes it far easier for them, when they want to learn to use a potty or a loo, to have a go; if they have seen you using this, anyway, it will be one of their aims.

## BABY'S FURNITURE AND EQUIPMENT

The need to feel polished and perfect and to want to surround the baby with the best that money can buy is one of the reasons why so much money is spent unnecessarily on glamorous new baby equipment. If it were fashionable to appear thrifty, this equipment would not be sold. There is a massive amount of barely used equipment around, and much of this can be bought second-hand extremely cheaply. I have never met anyone who wanted either to borrow or to buy secondhand who had any difficulty in finding what they wanted at a fraction of the new price. The pram and cot industry, however, operate a bit like the motor-car industry; every year new minor design adjustments are made which are supposed to provide a superior new model which is therefore the 'best' buy. On the whole, the Green parent can afford to ignore all this pressure, although just occasionally there is a breakthrough, such as the stroller from which baby can see mummy when they are out walking, instead of having to look in the opposite direction. But advances such as this are few and far between.

The Green parent also has the option on not buying certain items at all. It is not, for example, necessary to buy a plastic nappy-changing mat; a towel on a knee, or on the floor, does as well. Equally, it is not necessary to buy a cot or child-sized bed. Cots were designed for draughty houses. In most houses now it is not necessary to have the child above floor level and he can start with a mattress or futon on the floor, which also gives him more freedom and which completely eliminates the so-called problems attached to moving a child from cot to bed – problems which occupy a goodly space in the childcare manuals. If there are things he can play with when he wakes up, the child will not run around all over the house during the night or in the morning. He is also not subject to the demeaning procedure of standing up, holding on to his cot bars and calling for his parents (who become like gaolers with the power to free him) in the morning. When he needs to get up he can go and find them in a civilised, equal way.

## THE CREATION OF 'THEM AND US'

If we want our children to be a part of our world and share our values, the place we accord them in our lives, both mentally and physically, should reflect this desire. However, it is easy to be misled by oversold notions of the child's importance into basing our lives around him in a way that almost makes a mini-god of him. It is not fair on him; he does not need this responsibility. Mother-to-be is encouraged to do this; her advance preparation of the child's room is almost parallel to the construction of a shrine. Although this is an expression of love, the baby does not need it and would rather be around his family than separated in this way. The baby won't mind where he sleeps, except that ideally he'd like to be with his mother. For the mother not to bother appears, and can feel, negligent and uncaring. However, if the baby must have his own room, it would be more rational to decorate it in a style that the mother genuinely liked, since she may spend a lot of time in there and she, not the baby, will mind about it.

A typical catalogue picture of a baby's room shows it decorated in pale shades, the basic wallpaper being a delicate pattern on a white base – which will show every mark of a child's thumb. The floor is fitted with a pale, unpatterned carpet. High on the left-hand wall is a shelf holding a large array of bottles of various babycare lotions, a few picture books (quite inaccessible to any child under 12) and a few, also inaccessible, soft toys. On the floor under the shelf there is a white storage unit, on top of which there is another – accessible – soft toy, and a special, quilted, 'babychange' bag. Moving round, there is a window, which will be too high to see out of until the child is about six, curtained with pretty, wallpaper-matching material which will exclude no light and keep in no heat. Under the window is another storage unit, on top of which are three immaculately clean, folded towels. Next to the unit there is a not very comfortable, scratchy basket chair. Then the inevitable cot with pretty curtains over the head end, and a plastic 'bumper' with cartoon characters round the side. There are three other items of furniture in the room; a high chair, in which the child has recently eaten a meal; a quilted plastic mat with various nappy-related items and cosmetics on it; and a playpen, containing more soft toys and a soft ball.

There are two people in the picture, a child of about 12–15 months, standing in his playpen, holding on to the edge and looking out at his mother. He – or she? – is spotlessly clad in a yellow stretchy romper suit. The mother at whom he is looking is not over-enthusiastic; she is dressed in cream and white, has extraordinary flowing and feminine blonde hair, and is peering rather gingerly round a half-open door, as if to check on whether any servicing is needed at this moment. It is hard to tell whether she is coming or going, or why she is there at all, unless it is to ensure that she can safely leave him in the pen for a bit longer before he becomes frantic and she has to do anything about him.

This image of babycare is tragic. And that is not too strong a word. It is tragic because, as in true dramatic tragedy, the person who is supposed to be the hero of the piece has no control, and is imprisoned in sterility by the person who is supposed to love him most. The accompanying box contains a graphic account of what happens when a mother tucks up her baby for the night, illustrating an attitude that until recently was considered good practice.

She straightens baby's vest and covers him with an embroidered sheet and a blanket bearing his initials. She notes them with satisfaction. Nothing has been spared in perfecting the baby's room, though she and her husband cannot yet afford all the furniture they have planned for the rest of the house. She bends to kiss the infant's silky cheek and moves towards the door as the first agonised shriek shakes his body.

Softly she closes the door. She has declared war upon him. Her will must prevail over his. Through the door she hears what sounds like someone being tortured. Her continuum sense recognises it as such. Nature does not make clear signals that someone is being tortured unless it is the case. *It is precisely as serious as it sounds.*

She hesitates, her heart pulled towards him, but resists and goes on her way. He has just been changed and fed. She is sure he does not *really* need anything therefore, and she lets him weep until he is exhausted.

Jean Liedloff, *The Continuum Concept*

We shall never raise children with a high self-esteem and a cooperative outlook until confrontation and enforced separation are removed from the parenting, and the child's desire to be part of his parents' lives is respected. The tiny baby is happiest when held, and is safe in the basic, low-technology device of a simple canvas sling. This also does away with the 'need' for rocking and bouncing devices, since the child with a reasonably active parent will get any amount of moving, bouncing and rocking if he is simply attached to the parent while he or she gets on with life. Once the adult is used to it, there is almost nothing that cannot be done with a child in a sling, on the front, back, or hip – cooking, shopping, gardening, cinema trips, playing the tuba, all these and many other everyday activities can proceed as normal.

The baby demonstrates his need to get away when he starts to crawl. But even then he wants to be included. And if we want him to share our concerns later in life, there is every reason not to send him off to another world of cartoon characters and plastic toys, objects whose design we do not like and, indeed, find so shaming that we stuff them all out of sight the minute the child is in bed.

The Green parent is unlikely to make the child the only focal point in his life. Such a parent has his own aims, and is trying to work towards a better world, a better place for human beings to live in and in which genuinely to love, and with a greater chance of a future. His child has come into his universe, and is a vital part of it, both for his own sake and for the reinforcement he provides for his parents' efforts. But rather than abandon his efforts socially in order to create a children's world for his child, the parent allows the child to come with him on his own journey. This does not mean that the Green parent is necessarily out and about campaigning all the time – although many are, with babies in slings – but that he or she is leading a life which imparts a sense of caring, confidence, self-worth and outside purpose to the child. If the child has this sense, he will realise later on that his every action does affect the world, and can affect it positively or negatively. He sees his carer, his parent, living life and, at this stage of his life when he is basically in receipt of experiences and is unable to take an active part in them, the more he sees of life-enhancing activity the better.

## TOYS FOR TINIES

Alongside the sterilised babycare equipment that is sold to parents during this first year are toys. Many children's rooms are littered with jumbled-up toys that have barely been used, and the sight of a small child, disgruntled because he is apparently unable to find anything to do in a room that looks like a toyshop, will be familiar to many. There is everything, and yet there is nothing. The adult equivalent is dissatisfied 'grazing' with a TV zapper over several channels because there is 'nothing on'.

Actually, during the first few weeks of a child's life there is no need to have any toys at all. For her first six weeks the baby's concern is comfort or absence of discomfort. Feeding, sleeping, being cuddled are her major interests. After about six weeks she begins to be more interested in the world around her, and seems to like to look at things that are gently moving around, and to listen to sounds. But still, her best toy continues to be her carer.

She is still very sensitive to sudden noises or sudden changes in light. And she does not need 'stimulation' from other people; provided life is being lived, she will be watching it and trying to make sense of it. She will start inspecting bits of herself, such as her hands. She will often be happy to watch leaves blowing on trees.

A lot of mobiles are commercially produced for this age group. Many are unsuitable as they are at the wrong angle for the child to see. Some of them are fairly ugly, but not all; very beautiful ones are available. They can easily be made using natural materials such as leaves and pieces of cloth; if the child is to grow up with a sense of harmony it is worth making harmonious ones if others are not available. The simplest way is to run a piece of string across the room at a height where the baby can see it, and hang things from it.

As the child sits up and holds on to things, an enormous variety of toys, notably rattles, is available. Here again, there is no need to buy the commercial versions; there is endless fun to be had with old tubes, jars and boxes, which, with the help of the child, can be filled with beads or beans or milk-bottle tops, acorns, conkers, seeds from trees, and so on. There are some lovely rattles available on the market, such as a smooth basketry ball with a tinkly bell in it, but in general, aesthetic sensibility and commercial toys seem to have little connection.

By the age of about one, infants enjoy making things happen. Long before this, though, many of them will have had some kind of activity centre tied into their cot to help keep them amused in the morning. These are fairly dire. They are ugly to look at and contain a set of switches, buttons to press, dials and so on, that activate some kind of generally unpleasant noise (clicking, pooping, all the sounds that children are supposed to 'like' and which are in fact more likely than anything else to condition them to an acceptance of 20th-century cacophony). They could equally well be given a bamboo pipe down which they can blow to produce a pleasant sound, or a little bell, or a mirror, or an old, plain, telephone. And as the infant will enjoy making simple things happen using his hands as tools, almost anything which can have a hole on it can be threaded on a string and will spin when he bats at it. This allows the parent to put on the string images which he would like the child to grow up with (one cricketing freak I knew carved a beautiful miniature bat and ball for his small son).

During the latter part of the first year, catalogues will recommend that the child be bought a jump seat and a baby walker. In the jump seat the child is suspended from the doorway in a piece of canvas, and jumps up and down. But not only is it not clear what this will do for the child's back, but he would probably be as happy bouncing on an old mattress, a sprung cushion or, ideally, on somebody's knee. Bouncing is evidently great fun, but an undue emphasis on this kind of hype, as opposed to the gentler bouncing the child gets when carried about by his mother, seems quite unnecessary. Neither the bouncer nor the walker will particularly help the baby to walk. They may also, because of her feeling of mobility, lower her motivation to crawl, which is a stage of human development considered by many to be an important pre-walking activity (although there are infants who seem to leave it out altogether).

If a child is trying to be upright, the simple alternative to a baby walker is to arrange enough stable furniture for him to have something to hang on to as he cruises round the room. All kinds of different routes can be set up, using resources already available rather than buying in items whose use is limited. However, one item which does provide years of fun and use at this stage is the trolley, in which the child can move things around. This functional item, made of wood and metal, does not confine the child, and gives an enthusiastic walker the chance to help at home and to move things around. Another use, for children who like spinning things, is turning it upside down and setting the wheels in motion. It can later be used as a doll's buggy, as a scooter, as a storage place, as a trailer with the handles removed. And in this condition it becomes a pretend skateboard, or the base of a cardboard 'boat' in which the child can sit and row himself along: and even after all that use, it is fit to be passed on to somebody else.

## THE MOBILE CHILD

Once he is mobile, whether crawling or walking, the infant really does want to move. For months he has been dependent on others to fetch and carry for him, and to provide things to look at. When he can crawl he can begin to follow up his own interests, and will take very little looking after if he is allowed to do so. But he can only be allowed to do so if the home is childproofed. Breakable items should be out of reach, tempting items not left around, and cupboards that he can reach can have safety catches put on them. If he cannot open them all he will not mind, provided there are some cupboards and drawers he can empty; for example, he will love emptying and filling the bottom

remove handles

wood and metal trolley

boat shape made
from cardboard
box, stapled
to trolley

cloth or paper strips,
stapled or stuck to box,
to look like water,
and hide wheels

home-made
oars

*The trolley, and one of its many uses*

drawer of a chest of drawers, and investigating the contents. If the drawers are arranged so that the bottom ones contain stuff that will not suffer from his treatment (socks and knickers, for example, which may turn into hats during this adventure) and he is allowed to get on with it, he will enjoy himself happily and constructively for considerable periods of time. Although any mess may look hair-raising, it doesn't take long to clear up, and if the parent does it with him he gradually learns about the completion of a task. All for free. Similarly, if the bottom shelf or two of an open cupboard has on it unbreakable pots and pans, and perhaps the odd wooden spoon, he will enjoy those.

He often really begins to like water at this stage. Not only can he be given a washing-up bowl with lots of margarine tubs for boats, but he may also enjoy sitting in the kitchen sink while you do your chores. He may even, while in there, enjoy washing up the fruit squeezer and the cheese grater and any other interestingly shaped and textured unbreakable items.

In fact he will be interested in almost anything, and it is fun to put together a collection of small (not sharp or swallowable) items in a box for him to unload and inspect, and to move from container to container. Bits of cloth, old cotton-reels, flowerpots, crayons, balls, small balls of wool, little boxes, almost anything will do. The scope is wider if you have a child who does not automatically put everything in his mouth, because the safety problem is less. Commonsense and a knowledge of the child will dictate what should be avoided.

A few old magazines and newspapers are also useful. Since children do not read words at this stage, and many magazines have lovely pictures, you can 'read' these with him as well as anything else, and he will also 'read' them on his own quite happily. Newspapers serve another purpose – children from about one often love tearing them up. Although it was suggested to me that doing this could encourage destructiveness, the way they do it is more exploratory than destructive, and those several children I know who have done it have not become destructive.

This kind of calm, self-generated activity demonstrates how the child will stimulate herself and satisfy her own curiosity. The myth which needs debunking is that the child needs to be stimulated. We are told that if he is not, he will be bored. But nowhere in the texts is any distinction made between those times when the child may want just to be quiet, or to watch something, and when he is what adults call 'bored'. The consumer culture, in order to sell its goods, works hard through its various agencies of publicity to make people believe that they are hardly alive unless there are tangible events or material items filling up their lives all the time. And even an event barely exists unless there is something to prove it. Holidays often seem to exist as much in the photograph album or on the videotape as they do in the soul. One major London theatre takes more money from the sale of souvenirs of its shows than it does in ticket sales. Something has to happen, and something tangible should result – product replaces process once again. The child who lies on his back during a walk in the woods and looks up through the trees is thought of as rather unusual – he isn't getting anywhere. And the mother whose child wants to spend hours just looking out of the window may well be told there is something wrong with the child.

This mentality is cultivated by our own childhood and an education system in which we have become so used to being given things to do that it is hard to believe that a child could be happy without these things; not only are we not happy if we have nothing to do, but we may also feel guilty if we are not busy. To stay in bed in the morning until midday with a good book should not involve guilt; it is a non-destructive, energy-saving, regenerative process, but most of us would feel apologetic if we did it on a weekday. However we need to be able to credit the child with a tendency for reflectiveness and watching, since these go alongside his natural curiosity and imagination. His capacity to spend hours repeating the same activity demonstrates his tendency to master activities, his enjoyment of process and his lack of need for continual novelty.

When we reconsider where the child has come from, how he develops in the early months, and try to imagine actually being him, the possibility of overload becomes more obvious. The peace which he seeks initially is necessary for him to adjust gradually from the darkness of the womb to the astonishing level of inputs which face him in the world. Just looking round the room you are in now, as if for the first time; trying to make sense of all the items you can see, if it was for the first time, could take a very long time, rather like looking at the ceiling of the Sistine Chapel. The infant, unlike us, is unencumbered by context and association, and simply looks. And yet the culture does not want to give him time to look, for giving him this time sells no goods.

The culture tells us, generally speaking, that activity is preferable to apparent inactivity. If something is wrong, something else can be found to right it; so rather than removing action or object, we add more.

Then we wonder why our babies won't sleep. Firstly, they would rather sleep with us. Secondly, if we think of our own difficulties in sleeping on days when we have been bombarded with too many stimuli, we can understand the reasons for their not sleeping. We all need time for some calm (whether active or inactive) during the day. Animals know it, and plants know it. We know that the constant demands we have made on nature have deprived it of time for regeneration; the farmer who left a field fallow one year in three knew what he was doing, as did the inventors of the afternoon siesta.

The issue of balancing activity with regenerative, peaceful periods recurs throughout the whole of childhood and adult life. However, it is during the first year of childhood that the initial learning of parenting takes place, and it is also during this time that the child begins to understand the rhythms of the day. It is probably easier to establish a pattern and an outlook during this time than subsequently. So if we can sometimes enjoy ruminating and allow our children to do so, everybody's ability to find some inner peace and to discover and mobilise their own resources, without needing a box of props, will be enhanced.

## FURTHER READING

*The Continuum Concept*, Jean Liedloff, Penguin, London, 1986. Now a classic. It compares what she sees as basically uncaring western childcare with the rearing of children in the Yequana tribe of the Amazon basin. Extreme and brilliant. Because of the rain forest associations alone, it should be compulsory reading for all Greens. It has changed many people's attitudes to children, and was largely responsible for the spread of the baby sling. If I only recommended one book, this would be the one.

*The First Three Years of Life*, Burton White, Star, London, 1979. Paediatrician's commonsense view of maximising the child's use of these years.

*Baby and Child*, Penelope Leach, Michael Joseph, London, 1977. Much of the information is spurious, but some of the sections are invaluable and it is worth reading for these.

*The Anatomy of Judgment*, L. Johnson Abercrombie, Pelican, London, 1969. Looks at different physical and psychological perspectives, and the importance of these in our lives. It is not directly child related, but what it says really emphasises the importance of how points of view are developed in the early years.

*Ways of Seeing*, John Berger, Penguin, London, 1972. How the images presented to us affect our behaviour and attitudes.

# 3.
# GREEN KIDS ARE HEALTHY KIDS

## THE PLACE OF MODERN MEDICINE

The body is a remarkable piece of natural engineering. It contains within itself a self-righting ability which makes the technology of the self-righting yacht seem crude and clumsy. Yet what passes for healthcare seldom concerns itself with taking advantage of this ability. It is one of the industries in which high technology procedures and many possibly superfluous chemical treatments are to be found in greatest profusion.

There can be no question that many of the remarkable advances in medicine and medical technology have been of colossal benefit to humanity. Yet many advances which are ascribed to better medical technology, such as the fall in the perinatal mortality rate, are more correctly attributed to intermediate technology measures which have improved general health, sanitation and perinatal care. It is true that people live longer now than they did in the 1940s, but those who are now old had a childhood that was both more energetic and less chemically distorted than present-day children. We have no way at all of predicting the life expectancy of the modern child.

Before modern medicine developed, healing practices which involved the whole body and mind (and often related the rhythms of the body to the rhythms of the Earth) were, and still are, practised. Some of these, such as the laying-on of hands, require nothing additional to the presence of the healer; some use herbs in one form or another; some, such as acupuncture, use low-technology devices. The radical differences between most of these so-called 'alternative' practices and standard medical practice is that they treat the whole person rather than the isolated symptoms found in a person's body. They do not have a primary dependence on high technology and are therefore inexpensive in all but human resources. (For those who are still sceptical about the relationship of mind to chemical changes in the body, examples such as blushing when embarrassed or adrenalin racing round the bloodstream when nervous provide an easy demonstration of the links.) All these treatments require time and thought on the part of both the healer and the healed, and many of them require considerable effort on the part of the sick person. Such treatments have few, if any, adverse side effects on the person being healed; nor do they adversely affect the wider environment. Using these forms of cure does not rule out the use of ordinary medicine; often a combination of both can be effective. Many alternative practitioners do not shun allopathic (standard medical) treatment and will refer an individual to a hospital or suggest drug treatment if they think it might be advantageous, or if the body's own self-healing mechanisms seem inadequate. Conversely, a few mainstream general practitioners are beginning to recommend non-medical approaches.

The concept of health, as opposed to the treatment of illness, has begun to receive more general acceptance since mainstream practitioners have been forced to accept that alternative treatments, which promote health rather than alleviating symptoms, may work; they know that good health is the best weapon to use against illness. Good health does not necessarily imply a total lack of illness, but is a state of wellbeing in which bacteria, viruses and organic diseases are less likely to cause trouble than they do in an unhealthy body. When the World Health Organisation was founded after the Second World War it defined health as 'a state of complete physical, mental and social well-being, and not merely the absence of disease or infirmity'. Forty years on, there is still a long way to go.

Because of improved sanitation, antibiotics, inoculations and other preventive measures, diseases which threaten the individual today are no longer the major infectious disorders such as scarlet fever and smallpox. Diseases which are currently on the increase are arthritis, heart disease, arteriosclerosis, cancer, allergies, mental illness, premenstrual tension, blood sugar problems, stress symptoms and, in children particularly, chronic conditions such as glue ear and hyperactivity. To some extent these conditions are attributable to physical and psychological environmental factors. But to some extent each individual could also be held responsible for his own illnesses. However, not only does the culture provide environmental causes, but it also supports a medical establishment whose resources are devoted less to helping each individual control his own health than they are to providing for the establishment's own expansion.

The pattern of irresponsibility for health is set before birth. Before she has even delivered, the mother has had her responsibility for looking after herself undermined and, as we saw in Chapter 2, the benefits of the available high technology sold to her not as an option but as an advantage. Confidence is not created by dependence. If a person's confidence in her own ability to nurture herself is removed and the technological alternative presented as superior, she can hardly be expected to be confident about her ability to look after her own child's health (let alone the health of the planet). 'They' in authority have stated quite clearly that they know best. They have enshrined their knowledge in the statute book by, for example, making it illegal for a baby to be delivered without a qualified person being in attendance. Recently a husband and wife were taken to court for doing so, despite the fact that mother, baby and family were doing well. Although the law was presumably made to safeguard children, this baby did not need its protection. A costly prosecution such as this demonstrates the fear the medical establishment has of allowing individuals any responsibility.

From pregnancy onwards, mother becomes a patient, often under the supervision of a hospital, a technological institution processing people through its routines impersonally and quickly with the aid of drugs and disposable accessories. Baby is a product of hospital processes and once produced, he must, like other products of the industrial system, conform to certain standards.

Although initial tests at birth are useful indicators of problems that may arise later, which can be avoided if early action is taken, much of the subsequent weighing and measuring that takes place at regular intervals in the early months is as likely to alarm the mother as to help. Endless discussions can be overheard in clinics between mothers and health visitors, the latter providing reassurance that their baby's less-than-average weight gain this week is nothing to worry about. However, the worry was created in the mother's mind by the clinic's very own weighing machine and its published set of norms to which the baby is expected to conform. (These norms are themselves variable, anyway; the set in use at the time of writing was based on the average weight gains of bottle-fed babies, which would tend to be greater than the average gains of breastfed babies.)

Clinics may be desirable if they reduce a mother's sense of isolation and provide a local forum, which the best of them do. But the child's health is another matter. Most health visitors (and most mothers, if they would trust their own judgement) can tell by just looking at and holding a baby whether he is well or ill, just as a good midwife with an ear trumpet can judge a baby's heartbeat as efficiently as a heart monitor connected up to a woman in labour by an imprisoning strap.

We are not encouraged to trust our own judgement, though. For example, often if a baby or child (or adult) is ill, the first thing that happens is that his temperature is taken. We would learn more about the person's state of health – and his temperature — by staying with him, watching him and touching him, than by looking at a thermometer. A sudden rise in temperature is not hard to observe.

Maternity wards are trying to detechnologise their production process, but with their hands tied by the high-tech paradigm, they have to go through extraordinary contortions. One of their recent inventions is a birthing bed, an expensive and complicated mechanical device which hinges in the middle to help the mother get to her preferred delivery position – even sitting up. An old fashioned birthing stool, which can be made for about 1 per cent of the cost of a birthing bed, and a companion to support the mother, would produce the same effect. And it would be qualitatively infinitely superior, because it would involve the attention of a person and not the glories of a machine.

## RESTORING COMMON SENSE TO INFANT HEALTH

The rules of weights and measures are not the only ones which are given to the mother on her return home. One of the most notable concerns the heat at which the infant's house should be kept. The baby books suggest that the room temperature should be around 68 °F (20 °C); a typical statement is 'If your house cools off markedly during the night, the baby's room *must* be separately heated so that its temperature *never* falls below about 68 °F' (my emphases). How on earth do Eskimos survive? More seriously, houses have only very recently been kept at temperatures as high as these. The suggestion that the temperature must never fall below a certain level is quite extraordinary. Although a small baby born in a cold winter is vulnerable, the average baby is built to survive. The wastage of heat that must result from this approach, given the number of babies born daily, must make a significant contribution to the Greenhouse effect. If a parent really is that worried about her baby's ability to keep warm, having the baby in bed with her is an obvious solution.

Furthermore, it is only necessary to look at what happens to non-tropical plants and to pianos in overheated houses to be able to guess what might happen to a human being. Many adults who sleep in overheated rooms wake up with mild headaches and stuffy noses. People in overheated rooms at conferences, parties or offices often go for 'a walk in the fresh air to clear their heads'. Despite this, central heating at extremely high temperatures is now taken for granted. 'Putting on an extra layer' is considered rather old-fashioned, although those who do end up warm but not stuffy. No, the heating is turned on instead, consuming a huge amount of fuel, leaving us with massive heating bills and denying the body its capacity to adjust.

For my second birth, at home, we were told to have our delivery room heated to 80 °F, which we achieved after much diligent examination of a room thermometer. During my labour I thought I would die of perspiration. And as soon as the doctor arrived he said it was all quite unnecessary; 'All we need' he said, as he opened the windows, 'is heat quickly available if required.' He was one of a practice of doctors who applied commonsense principles to healthcare, while respecting the parent's anxieties.

Parents are quite naturally anxious; for example, there can be few situations as alarming to a new parent as a tiny baby with a cold. She breathes in irregular gulps, and often sounds as though the next breath will be the last. It is reassuring to see a doctor, and very tempting to give the infant one of the much advertised proprietary medicines which are readily available over the counter. It is also quite easy to give more than is necessary; in the case of a cold, some nose drops are so effective in helping the child to breathe that, if the cold continues, it may feel more caring to go on giving them than to stop. But within two days of use, the child can become dependent on them and be unable to breathe without them. So the less the better, very often.

What cannot be sold (and what would actually reduce the power of the medical establishment) is the idea of personal nursing care as cure. Dr Jolly, a paediatrician, did an experiment in which some sick babies in his hospital were given extra nurses, one each to carry them around all the time, while a control group received 'normal' treatment in bed. The carried babies recovered much more quickly than the others. It is easy to see why, if we view illness from our own perspective. The feeling of being cared for without fuss gives us a positive self-image. We feel worthy. We do not have to go on being ill; the attention we need is there to help us get better. Care is the cure.

Clearly many conditions need more than just care. But even if an illness needs drugs or technological treatment, care will help the technology to do its work. And the simple non-drug therapies often provide an inbuilt element of care; in the case of a child's cold, for example, symptoms can be relieved by creating a steamy environment for him, and by massaging his back with eucalyptus oil.

The medical establishment is loath to examine environmental variables when analysing changes in illness patterns. Glue ear, for example, could well be manufactured by the environment in which the sufferer lives. This condition seems to be related to catarrh, and results in sometimes quite severe, theoretically temporary, deafness, since the eardrum is blocked up with sticky glue-like material. Dr Jolly says that the change from the 'old type of otitis media leading to a runny ear with pus' to the now more common glue ear is 'believed to result from the wider use of antibiotics for infections in general, and the fact that in the case of ear infections the course of treatment is often not completed'. (If courses of antibiotics are stopped earlier than specified, there may be organisms left over which have been exposed to the antibiotic, and will have learnt in part how to be resistant to it.) And this could undoubtedly be one of the reasons, but it is very narrow reasoning. Many children who have either not had antibiotics or who always complete their courses get glue ear just the same. Now, instead of looking outside medical guidelines for possible environmental or dietary causes of glue ear, one of the standard procedures used when decongestant medicines have failed is to pierce the child's eardrum and to insert grommets (tiny plastic drain holes) to drain it. This is now a routine operation (as tonsillectomies were in the 1950s) despite the fact that the grommets can come out and often don't relieve the symptoms at all. What will be the next fad?

So it is well worth the Green parent's while to find out if there are any non-drug or low-tech remedies for any condition. A case study of a glue ear sufferer follows for two reasons; firstly, it is a common condition; and secondly, because this case demonstrates the way one family embarked on a do-it-yourself approach. The same method could be applied to other conditions.

When Zoe's parents suddenly became aware that three-year-old Zoe, who had always had a tendency to vagueness, was actually very deaf, they were quite worried. They went to doctors. She was prescribed decongestant medicine, which did nothing except make her vaguer (antihistamines tend to have this effect). She was looked at in a hospital, which recommended grommets or a tonsillectomy. Zoe's parents wanted neither. By chance, they happened to meet somebody else whose child had had a similar condition, and who told them what no doctor had said, which was that the problem was in some way related to catarrh.

Off they went and bought a book about catarrh, and discovered that it was one of the body's defence mechanisms for dealing with attacks on the nasal passages. Zoe had spent much of her life in overheated rooms with people who smoked, so that provided two clues to the causes. The book they were reading suggested that there were certain foods which could be 'mucus provoking', notably milk and sugar. That provided another clue; Zoe, although not a sugar-eater, was a copious milk-drinker.

So they decided that the obvious course of action was to alter Zoe's environment and diet – no smoke, lots of fresh air, extra exercise outdoors, no milk and no sugar. Within a few weeks the condition had started to improve significantly, although helpful friends kept on telling Zoe's parents that 'grommets had transformed their children overnight'. They knew what they were doing might take a long time. They also knew that after a few years Zoe's Eustachian tubes would in any case expand and that that would also help. Since Zoe appeared to be suffering neither intellectually nor socially, they felt that time could take its course. It took about three or four years of repeating the same treatment every time she had a cold, when catarrh threatened to invade, to clear the condition. However, not only had the condition gone by the time she was eight, but Zoe had become aware that her own health and the treatment of illness was something in which she could play an active part.

Zoe's parents continue to believe in the usefulness of doctors, whom they consult principally for diagnoses, regarding any 'cure' as being largely in their own hands. They are on safe ground, because they have been fortunate enough to find a good doctor, one of the increasing number who regard themselves as part of a therapeutic partnership with the 'patient' (partner) and who do not consider these partners cranks or traitors if they use self-help methods. Green parents would do well to find such a doctor.

However, many doctors are still not entirely happy about the use of dietary, herbal and homeopathic remedies, even though homeopathy is now available on the National Health Service. And unfortunately, just as the medicinal qualities of certain plants are beginning to be acknowledged, even by the orthodox medical profession, many of these plants are disappearing as the rainforests in which they grow are razed to the ground. If the demand for medicinal plants could be dramatically increased and the income from their sales thus raised, the preservation of the rainforests would be marginally more in the interests of their owners than is currently the case.

The wholistic approach to health and the use of non-chemical resources, with high technology solutions available as a last resort, is thus connected in several ways to the Green approach to life. Health, in Green thinking though, is more a question of prevention than of cure, and so its basic foundations are lifestyle and diet.

## CHILDREN EATING

Standard medical training does not devote a high proportion of its time to consideration of diet, so few doctors routinely ask their patients either about their lifestyle or their diet when they arrive in the surgery with minor ailments. And it is partly their training that has made the pharmaceutical industry one of the most profitable and powerful international industries, whose power includes a huge publicity machine busy convincing doctors and laymen of the virtues of its products. Given such opposition, it is not easy to place one's faith in the whole health approach, which is diet and lifestyle based.

We need to attend to our children's diets (and our own, for we are both their role models and their providers of breastmilk), for the sake both of our children and the world. The standard old-fashioned British diet was based on 'meat and two veg' and most

Having spent many years in hospital practice followed by eight years in the pharmaceutical industry I enthusiastically prescribed all the latest medicines. The more drugs I prescribed, the more patients I saw and the more patients I saw, the more drugs I prescribed. I paid little attention to nutrition until I attended a meeting of the McCarrison Society. I then began to look much more closely in to the field of nutrition, and by advising patients accordingly, the morbidity in my practice began to fall very significantly. I made further progress when I accompanied the advice with a persuasion to stop smoking.

Dr Hugh Cox, TD, MB, MRCGP, DCH, DRCOG,
from *TheWhole Health Manual*, Patrick Holford

of the advice given to parents used to revolve round the standards implied by this basic diet. Recently, though, standards have begun to change. Red meat is to be eaten only occasionally; going to work on an egg is bad for you (if you don't have a heart attack you'll have salmonella poisoning); salads are a Good Thing; and being a vegetarian doesn't automatically raise a lot of eyebrows. But despite these changes in prescribed adult standards (or perhaps because of them), parents are under more pressure to 'do things' to food or to buy processed, baby-food versions to feed their children.

'Why do porridge when there's Breakfast Timers ... there's plenty of vitamins and minerals stashed away inside every pack.' At a price, though, and in its wasteful packaging. Why not do porridge? It only takes minutes, and the whole family will enjoy it. There may even be positive health reasons for serving it (see box).

## PORRIDGE HAS MORE HEART

An old-fashioned bowl of porridge is the medical profession's latest weapon against heart disease. Doctors at King's College Hospital in London found that a plate of oats in the morning – along with a low-fat diet – helped to reduce cholesterol levels by as much as 6 per cent.

*Daily Express*, 12 April 1989

We are almost too well aware now of the foods which we should not give to our children, which might cause them to develop an allergy or some other chronic condition. Wheat and cow's milk are two known baddies. All the warnings, coupled with our insecurity and lack of knowledge, has put us in the hands of baby-food manufacturers, whom we assume must be experts and will therefore provide the best possible nutrition. But what is in their food?

You can buy three and a half jars of banana pudding for babies from four months for £1 (to buy the so-called health food version will cost you three times as much). These three and a half jars contain water, sugar, bananas, full cream milk powder, thickeners (modified starch, manioc starch), stabiliser (carob bean gum) and vitamin and mineral mix (a list of which is on the label). Since the two principal ingredients of this concoction are water and sugar, it is hard to see any reason for buying it. To give a child a banana is not difficult, even if it involves mashing up half a ripe one with a little milk and sugar, or perhaps yoghurt. This kind of processed product both generates packaging and costs a great deal. So why does anybody buy it?

One of the reasons is that 'moving a child on to solids', rather like 'moving a child from cot to bed', has become a discipline all of its own. The whole business of when a child should first have solid food, how it is given to him, how it is combined with breast or bottle-feeding, has become a matter for experts. Baby books sometimes suggest a weight that the child will reach after which he should be given solid food – although 'for the first 6 months a baby needs only extra vitamin D to cover all his nutritional needs'. (Here I would like to refer the reader back to page 28 and ask whether the child with plenty of exposure to natural sunshine and not too many baths would need even this supplement to avoid the risk of rickets.) But we are then told not to leave solid foods this late. 'She should start tastes of solid food by her fifth month anyway. If you leave the new experience until she is much older than this, she may find the new tastes and feeding methods hard to accept.'

This and much similar advice assumes that the child is not programmed to seek what she wants and that the mother is not tuned in, or cannot be tuned in, to her child. At some point a child starts chewing, whether or not he has teeth. Presumably this is nature's indication that he wants something to chew. But instead of being told to wait for this moment, or for some other sign from the child, we are given an age and a rule. Why don't we simply feed some of our own food, unsalted, to babies (salt is bad for them), rather than follow instructions to prepare or buy strained foods or cereals?

But the child who is ready for more than milk may want to chew. Obviously the toothless jaw cannot deal with the same food that mature teeth can handle, but it is ludicrously expensive and time consuming to mess about with baby foods. Babies who are given a piece of potato, pear or peach will have a go. If they are sitting up at table on an adult's knee and want food, they will go for the food. Most of the feeding rigmarole, with its special little plastic dishes and rather badly designed plastic spoons with which an adult shovels food into a baby, makes more work rather than less and, more importantly, denies the child the chance to act naturally.

Neglected old Mother Nature can and does show us the way to let our children eat (forget the notion of feeding) if we let her. If the child is with adults, at least for daytime meals, he will gradually take an interest in the food and reach for it. Mother may need an apron at this point, but baby may not need a bib because much of the food he can hold easily will not soak his surrounding world in the spattery way that spoonfuls of liquid mush would. He will, of course, happily pick up mush in his hands, and then his clothes will need some coverall protection. But eventually he will want to use cutlery, and if he can see adults using it he won't need teaching. When he does decide to try, an ordinary short-handled coffee-spoon is far easier for the child to use himself than the normal unwieldy, specially made long-handled affair which keeps mother's hand at a good distance from baby's mouth while he tries to suck slops off it.

People who follow their own child's 'feeding method', which is not really a method at all, reckon not to have the all-too-common eating problems with their children. Indeed, by definition they cannot, since the child is leading the way and organising his own eating. It is cheaper, simpler and more inclusive for the child and the parent than serving goo to a child strapped into a separating restraining device.

What we ourselves eat, and therefore give children to eat, is obviously important. One manufacturer of baby foods suggests 'You could start your baby off with Bone and Beef Broth, then by 7 months she could be tucking into Country Lamb with Carrots, and at 15 months enjoying Farmhouse Steak Dinner' all designed with increasingly large lumps for the growing infant. So you could; it would be a tasty diet for the meat-eater. But it makes no sense at all to serve it out of overpriced tiny tins, jars or packets. Mother may object that she needs them because baby has his main meal at lunch and she does not; in which case the obvious thing for the parents to do is to have their home-cooked lamb with carrots for their evening meal, and save a bit for baby to have the next day. Not only is this system efficient and cheap, but the mother has control over what goes into the food, and the baby will get used to her cooking.

There is currently a national debate about what kinds of food are safe and what are not. It is clear that many food items can do more damage to the developing organism (the baby) than they do to the adult. It would therefore seem sensible to try to buy as much genuinely organically grown fresh food as possible, both if the baby is breastfeeding and when he starts to eat solid food, simply because nobody really knows the long-term effects of adulterated food. Organic produce costs more, but health comes at a price – and in any case organic food prices will not fall until there is sufficient demand to increase supply. If we demand enough of it now, and pay for it, our children will be able to get it more easily and cheaply when they are having their own children.

Whether the baby is brought up vegetarian or not should depend on whether the parents are vegetarian, assuming they are including her in their life. There are problems with babies on vegan diets, which are hard to balance correctly. Veganism has caused malnutrition in babies, although if very carefully thought out a vegan diet can work. Clearly bringing up vegetarians is doing the planet a favour, since it takes about 15 kilograms of grain to produce 1 kilogram of meat, and the grain would feed far more people if used directly.

It is difficult to find foods on the mass market, either vegetable or animal, which have not been chemically treated, but it is worth seeking them out not only for their health value but for their taste. A fresh, organically grown carrot bears about as much resemblance to the standard commercial carrot as the best Assam does to instant tea; many children will reach adulthood without knowing the difference, if we do not start them young.

There is no baby food on the market which needs to be bought at all, although it is certainly useful if you are travelling to be able to buy the odd jar of this or that. If your child is an inveterate nibbler, cut up fruit or vegetables can be kept in a dark, airtight container, or a tin of home-made rusks (extra toast made at breakfast time, stood up to make it crisp, and cut into strips) kept at hand. The child, as an eater, is one of the family. If the family is well-fed and eats as a unit, the child will eat well.

Our grandmothers would have told us all this. The mothers of those of us who are now middle-aged try to tell us; they brought us up just after the last war, when food was in very short supply and before the chemical agrarian revolution had taken place. The nation as a whole has never been healthier. And the recipe was amazingly simple; a reasonable variety of plain foods in smallish quantities, plenty of fresh air, exercise and sleep, and a purpose in life, that of rebuilding the nation for peacetime. It is only since the postwar onset of mass consumption, the lack of a good reason to be healthy and the search for constant novelty, that we have forgotten simple health rules and been encouraged to buy 'cures' at the chemist instead. One nutritionist, who had worked for six years with children, said a decent diet, with enough exercise and sleep and good social relations, would have kept most of the children he saw well clear of the doctors' waiting rooms. But this is not the child of today: instead he is overfed with chemical junk food, sits in front of the television or computer instead of using his body, stays up late to watch another programme, and lives in a family isolated from any real community so that the visit to the doctor is welcomed by his mother, serving as it may as a substitute for a chat with a friend.

It is a sorry state of affairs, and it is not necessary. We know, and have always intuitively known, about diet and health. However the culture has encouraged us to forget what we knew and to accept the instant 'solutions' that it has sold to us. There are people whose housing and environmental conditions make it more or less impossible to contemplate good health; these conditions should be improved as a priority. Those of us who are in a more fortunate position owe it to ourselves as well as to our children to resist what may seem at first sight the easy option, and to take a little time out organising our diet and daily routines in a health-promoting way. Initially this will take more time and effort than buying commercial alternatives or drugs, but once our outlooks and routines have been reorganised, the better option takes no longer, gives us more energy, uses less resources, generates less waste and has less harmful side effects.

As with all other issues considered in this book, there will be compromises. The occasional Mars bar is a great treat, and does not do untold damage. Nor does the odd paracetamol. It is really a question of shifting the balance and making instant foods and occasional drugs the exception rather than the rule. The human organism can survive these exceptions, and the planet can stand the odd bit of prepackaging. But children's health is not standing up well to its excessively chemical diet, and landfill sites are beginning to groan under the volume of plastic they are receiving. We should be a healthier world with less of both.

## DEALING WITH MINOR ACHES AND PAINS

The following list of suggestions for everyday healthcare and emergencies was given to me by a practising GP with standard medical qualifications, who uses drugs both at home and in her practice only as a last resort. She, however, emphasises the need for each person to find out what works best for them.

- For occasions when you would normally take aspirin or paracetamol, give a plateful of finely chopped raw cabbage and have a brief lie down. (Make a coleslaw dressing with olive oil, cider vinegar and a couple of teaspoons of sweet French mustard, add garlic, herbs and seasoning to taste and shake hard in a jar.) If you keep junior paracetamol in the house, it should be the smallest possible bottle. In her family, raw vegetables are served at the beginning of every meal. There is much evidence that this is an extremely sound basic health-promoting habit.
- Bruises, aches and pains – keep a pot of Tiger Balm (available from good health food stores and many chemists) for rubbing in. Children love it – it's reassuring stuff.
- Open wounds – Dettol and plasters. Also keep a few crêpe bandages in the house, but if you use safety pins with them make sure they are rolled up in the middle where children won't get them and they won't get lost.
- Wounds, bruises or burns – arnica helps quicker healing.
- If diet really is good and varied, supplements are not necessary. However, it is very hard to be consistent about diet and to know whether foods contain adequate quantities of vitamins by the time they reach the purchaser. If you are in any doubt, give a daily vitamin and mineral pill – only one,

too much can be toxic. Better safe than sorry.

- Onset of infections – give lots of extra vitamin C preferably in fresh fruit and vegetables.
- Coughs and colds – relieve symptoms with menthol and eucalyptus oil, available from health food stores and chemists, in a bucket of steamy water. The sufferer puts a towel over her head and breathes in the vapours. This oil may also be put on pillows and handkerchiefs. The sort we use is called Olbas, and in steamy water clears the entire head in minutes. Rub Vick into chest and back. An old-fashioned vaporiser (by Wrights, available at large chemists) keeps bedroom air moist at night. Make sure the central heating in bedrooms is turned off. Drink lots of water and cut out mucus-promoting fatty foods.
- Hay fever and similar conditions – commercial homeopathic preparations are effective for many, and are available at health food stores and some chemists.
- If something poisonous is swallowed, which happens even in the most careful of households, make an egg nog with a raw egg, milk, sugar and flavouring, drink it immediately and then go to Casualty with the container the poison was in so they can identify it. Salmonella infection is unlikely if the egg is genuine organic free-range. And anyway, it is more easily curable than the results of swallowed household cleaner, for example.
- Use the doctor wisely, and always take a pencil and paper to the surgery with you to write down what he said. If you are using him for diagnosis rather than treatment, you need to have a precise diagnosis so that you can be more accurate in finding an alternative remedy. Try to find a doctor who prefers not to prescribe anything, if this does not mean too much travelling. Ideally, a doctor should be within easy walking distance. You might like to contact a naturopath for occasional visits.
- Genuine healing takes time. Many ailments for which, for example, antibiotics are prescribed are self-limiting (anti-biotics merely speed up the process). As far as possible, if the ailment will clear itself up, try to let it. Talk to your doctor about this.
- Study a first aid book or do a first aid course. This will prove useful to you on all kinds of occasions, and will only take about six hours in total.

## FURTHER READING

*The Whole Health Manual*, Patrick Holford, Thorsons, Wellingborough, 1983. Basically an explanation of health promoting nutrition. For specific ailments health food stores and many chemists stock a variety of short books.

*The Encyclopaedia of Natural Medicine*, Michael Murray and Joseph Pizzorno, Macdonald Optima, London, 1990. This deals generally with natural medicine and looks specifically at a wide variety of health problems.

*Holistic First Aid – A Handbook for the Home*, Dr Michael Nightingale, Macdonald Optima, London, 1989. This has many interesting ideas.

*Family Health — Care and Management At Home*, Robert Andrews and Kirk Hargrave, Sphere, London, 1978. Has useful tips on understanding standard medical practices and choosing from various schools of thought.

The following three books look at the wider considerations of modern so-called health practice.

*Chemical Children*, Peter Mansfield and Jean Monro, Century Hutchinson, London 1987. How to protect your family from harmful pollutants. This is a slightly alarming but very informative book.

*Cured to Death*, Arabella Melville and Colin Johnson, New English Library, London, 1982. Deals with the damaging side effects of many modern drugs.

*Medical Nemesis – The Expropriation of Health*, Ivan Illich, Calder & Boyars, London, 1975. An eye opener. If you need an incentive to look after your health, this book provides it. It has changed the lives of many people.

# 4.
# TODDLERHOOD

## THE AGE OF EXPLORATION

The first 15 months are over. In the place of the passive infant is a possibly walking, embryonically talking, energetic explorer, taking in with an alert ear and eye actions and expressions which she will shortly be able to imitate with uncanny accuracy. She is looking at the adult from a new perspective as she develops an obvious mind of her own and, while this is a welcome development, it can make life seem very hard work at times.

She has had her first birthday, which hopefully has been duly celebrated, for birthdays are part of the rhythm of the child's and the family's life. Although there may have been too many adult and child guests at the party for her to cope with, and she may have ended the afternoon in tears because it was all too much, it will have meant something to the adults and older children. What she is left with is a pile of new toys, which may be confusing to her. Fortunately, until the child is about three, her parents are still able to remove excess toys surreptitiously for later use without the child noticing.

Toys are fun. Every child needs a few because they keep her happily and harmlessly occupied. But toy manufacturers want us to buy more than our child needs. Unwittingly aided by developmental guides, they invite us to begin to worry about our child's intelligence, coordination and development. And the culture, both locally and globally, does not help us to be at ease. Locally, somebody else's child is said to have read his first word, hopped her first step, or completed a puzzle designed for three-year-olds. Other mothers are asked to admire this great achievement, which is often declared to have been made possible by the aid of a wonder toy, method or gadget such as the baby walkers mentioned earlier. Globally, books on parenting carry warning messages on their covers like 'From birth to three your child has most to learn', so that we begin to wonder what might happen to her if she misses out before she is three. What is it, anyway, she is supposed to be learning?

We ask what we can do to help, for we have been conditioned for years to assume that learning also involves active teaching, and at this stage we, the parents, are the teachers. The answers are provided for us. 'Postman Pat's Playschool – for 2–6 year-olds, the most vital learning years. They think they're playing – you know they're learning.' You can buy this for only a few pounds a month by standing order, which sellers well know are only infrequently cancelled. Book Club advertisers tell you 'How you fill this space:'

depends on 'How you fill this space:'

Or 'Bloks is a new range of play and learn toys for children from one to six years . . . simple words and sums, pictures, shape sorting, all for only £15.99 – or you can buy a very small pack from £4.99.' And we worry that we'd better get something, or our children will miss out on one or more aspects of their development.

---

We know how important it is to encourage toddlers to look and listen, touch and hold. Colours, sound, textures, weights, fragrances, the earliest experiences are the most formative and our toys make the most of babies' ability to learn from play.

from a toy catalogue

---

We are presented with statements such as 'hammering is an *essential* activity', which is obviously a straightforward lie.

'Other faculties will be enhanced', with easy miniature puzzles, shape sorting games, posting boxes and all the rest. Many of these toys, particularly the wooden ones, are well made and beautiful, but more are not. One of the best selling ranges of toys is made in garishly coloured plastic and seems designed to infantilise, which is not what the child needs. For example, their periscope, instead of just being what it is, has a face on it; the whole range makes the implicit statement that children need to be pandered to and that they do not deserve the same aesthetic standards as adults. And this range is not even particularly cheap.

The catalogue quoted in the box makes one serious mistake, which anyone who knows anything about children will probably spot, and that is to suggest that children have to be actively encouraged to use their senses. A trip to the supermarket provides plenty of examples of mothers who have to discourage their children from looking and listening, touching and holding. 'Don't say how fat that lady is when she can hear.' 'Yes, I know he's got a funny voice, but don't say so.' 'It may be pretty but PUT IT DOWN!' The child's whole being is oriented towards observation and discovery, if she has not been deterred during her first year. The only way she can make sense of her universe, now that she is beginning to see herself as a separate being, is to explore it. And she will learn more if she can follow up her own interests than if she is given prescribed toys – just like an adult, who is more likely to remember the results of her own enquiries than to remember gratuitously given information that is spurious to her needs at the time. Much so-called encouragement, offered in the form of specially provided playthings, is essentially a message from adults about what they want the child to do. The playthings can block her interest in her immediate surroundings, so she may end up able to do a complicated puzzle but still be in the dark about how a meal gets to the dining-table.

To know about, and to be able to act on, the local environment is empowering to both child and adult. A two-year-old chopping marrows for the evening meal is being allowed to develop more of an 'I can affect things' outlook on life than the child watching Postman Pat on a video. She will never be able to affect Postman Pat. If we follow the notion of acquiring information that facilitates action and the ability to act through to an adult level, there are clear parallels. For example, watching national TV news may be globally informative, but there is little any of us can do about it, and we may just end up feeling powerless and depressed. On the other hand, if we know what is happening locally, we can bend the ear of Sid Smith, our local councillor, and get things changed. Our situation will be improved and we will feel good about our own abilities. Many figures who are now getting things done on a national level started at the local level; success in small-scale activities led to the ability to succeed on a larger scale.

Taking local action requires local knowledge. The child's first drive to exploration is in the home. He wants, and needs, to know all about it. As far as the Green parent is able, it pays, to quote Burton White, to 'Make all safe and leave him to get on with it.' This is not an invitation to the child to wreck the home. Some areas can be kept out of bounds (a bolt near the top of the door sorts this out). One commonsense child writer was in favour of having one great big 'No' item in each room so that the children would learn to be careful, and to respect what was there. This seems quite a good idea, although I personally was too lazy to administer such a rule and put all the Noes out of the way until later. This also meant I didn't have to supervise visiting children who might have different Noes. I was, however, convinced of the value of this idea by a stringed instrument maker who followed the No rule so that his children could safely be allowed into his workshop, as a result of which they were remarkable craftspeople at a very early age and knew about the care required in handling delicate objects.

The more scope the child has to explore and improvise, the less she needs in the way of actual toys. A favourite activity at this age, for example, is unpacking bookshelves. Like the infant's sock drawer, it is possible to have one or two such shelves accessible. If similar access is available throughout the in-bounds areas of the home, the exploration of colours, sounds, textures, weights and fragrances which the toy catalogue mentions will take place quite naturally, especially if children are allowed to handle soap and other household smells, are allowed to go in the garden, are in the room when the parent gets out the rag bag, and join in food preparation. Furthermore, the colours of food and flowers, the colours of nature, their smells and textures are far less likely to desensitise the child than the harsh colours and uniform texture of many toys.

## BOOKS AND READING

Lack of subtlety in colouring is also a feature of many children's books. Much reading can still be done with the same material as that mentioned in Chapter 2, and at this age the child can help to make loose-leaf 'books' using cut-outs and postcards. If you want her to get used to the look of words, you can write 'The sea', or even a sentence or two, next to the picture in the home-made book. Although a lot of children's books are lovely, there is no reason for children's entire literary experience to depend on what is commercially created specially for them. As well as reading their own books, they will often want to look at whatever appears to fascinate their parents, and they will reject it if it has no meaning for them. I once went to an exhibition of the work of Le Corbusier, most of which was models, designs and pictures of buildings – not an exhibition for children, for whom nothing 'suitable' was provided – and was really struck by the large number of very small children who were obviously really enjoying looking at the exhibits (and were presumably 'learning' at the same time, even if they were not learning what was being taught).

At this age the child is thought to be unable to distinguish between fantasy and reality. If she is told a story, it doesn't matter whether it is truth or fiction. Nor will she make much sense of a storyline. What she assimilates, particularly from looking at actions and pictures, is a set of images which she will have lost from her conscious mind by the time she is about six or seven. But although lost to the conscious mind, the images that the child is assimilating will later form part of the unconscious basis of her conscious judgments and actions (which is why psychotherapists are interested in trying to get their clients to recover some of these memories).

We know, for example, that people reared in round huts with no experience of standard western geometric form, perceive perspective differently to westerners. Similarly, somebody brought up on musical intervals smaller than a semitone, which is our minimum distance between two notes, 'hears' differently. Since early experiences and perceptions are accepted without analysis or judgment and yet form the basis for judgment later in life, parents have some responsibility for ensuring that they expose the child to images which give her a sense of harmony against which she can measure later experiences. If she is presented with the grotesque and the distorted, this, like the noise of the activity centre, will seem acceptable to her.

Verbal as well as pictorial images count. The parent has the widest choice of acceptable verbal images when he invents his own stories. However, the proliferation and high quality of many children's books can make it seem pointless and daunting to a parent to tell a story without a book in his hand. There are two good reasons why this fear is worth overcoming, and why telling a story is as valuable as reading one. Firstly, reading from a book is an example of the dependence of our imaginations on somebody else's text and illustrations, so the model for the child is of parent as narrator rather than creator. Secondly, it is much easier to look the child in the face and really share the story, without a book in hand.

Do we really have it within ourselves to make up our own stories? It sometimes seems hard to believe that our children might like our stories as much as, say, the Ahlbergs'. Yet Daddy's day in the office is a story. And he may possibly find a more eager listener in his child than in his wife, particularly if he can talk about the cleaner who's just leaving to have a baby, and the saga of the failed coffee machine, and what he felt this morning when he was greeted by mountains of paper. Some people find, to their surprise, that after conquering their initial fears and starting 'Once there was a little girl, whose name was ... One day she saw an ambulance outside her window ...' that the story just rolls on. Or 'Once there was a fish in a great big blue sea and he lived with his mum, Mrs Herring, and his dad, Mr Herring ...' and then endless adventures ensued as they tried to escape from the fishing boats. Plot doesn't matter much.

Many adults have a fund of stories stored in the back of their minds. Simple nursery rhymes tell stories, and can easily be elaborated. What did Jack and Jill look like? What did they wear? Why did Jack fall down? There are myths, legends, Bible stories, many of which have been forgotten in detail but can easily be revised. Many of our own favourite stories may not be available in children's book form, anyway, and our children enjoy sharing our favourites. I remember being eagerly told the long and complicated story of Wagner's cycle of operas, the Ring of the Nibelungs, by a four-year-old whose father's enthusiasm had led him to share it with her.

And if you want an ecological slant to storytelling and books, there are many books on the market which can be read or which will help you to make up stories. Animal stories are always popular with children, although rather too many of them put animals in human dress and ignore their animal characteristics. And there are some plant books, although very few stories with plants as heroes (the Flower Fairies series is an exception, and does bring over the character of each plant).

## THE MOBILE CHILD IN THE HOUSEHOLD

In a way our lives are more constrained by our small mobile children than they are when they are in the pre-mobile phase. The child is less portable than she was, and although she can be carried in a rucksack-type frame on the shoulders, is less likely to fall asleep when she has had enough of wakefulness. She needs a more definite structure to her day. On the other hand, although more of life may have to be spent at home, her contribution to the household increases significantly. Very small children can learn to wash up, to load and unload the washing machine (which will take them ages as they enjoy doing it so much), to handwash clothes and other items, to clean (a two-year-old with a couple of cloths will sometimes leave a basin looking as if it had been French-polished), to begin to cook – a blunt knife will cut a mushroom, or they can break it by hand, and other foodstuffs can be cut and stirred, or poured or spooned out of their packets. We ate a lot of fresh peas when our children were small because they loved shelling them as their contribution.

Often the child can do much more than we believe, and if she is given the chance to try will do very well. She is also prepared to accept that there are things that she cannot yet do. She may not always finish a job, and she may do it very slowly, but she can do it. And it doesn't have to be turned into a 'fun' event. The satisfaction a child can derive from doing necessary or contributory jobs is the kind of satisfaction an adult can derive from gardening or DIY or anything else that they know is needed, important and creative. The doing of the job brings its own reward. Nor is it necessary, or even desirable, to tell a child how good and clever she is when she is being useful. It is patronising. She is good and clever anyway, and wants to help. It shows more respect for her abilities to express delight at the job done and to thank her in the same way that an adult would (hopefully) be thanked. It is equally unhelpful to her to say a job is wonderful if it is not, and simply thanking her for her work renders such a judgment redundant. If it really is very good, then of course she should know. But at this stage what matters is her inclusion as a contributor.

## LEARNING TO COPE WITH THE RESULTS OF ACTIONS

By now the child has sufficient experience to begin to see the consequences of his own actions. He can see that jobs need finishing, and that it is a good idea to do what his parents do, not to leave his detritus around to get broken or for somebody else to clear up. (This aspect of task completion is emphasised in Montessori teaching.) He should be encouraged to regard clearing up as a part of the process of an activity. He can also be allowed to clear up accidents rather than watching somebody else doing so. Many children grow up feeling guilty about spilt things, and therefore ignore them. If a child accidentally spills a drink, she has done nothing wrong. Both her foresight and her coordination are not yet fully developed, although the more drinks she has been allowed to handle, the less likely she is to spill them. She will not be unhappy to help mop up if the adult present calmly gets a couple of cloths and allows her to join in. She learns about clearing up – that she can do it for herself, that it is easy and that she does not have to feel guilty about her messes.

It would, however, be unfair and unrealistic to expect her to clear up a roomful of toys and other bits and pieces on her own (this is also an argument for not having too many toys). But she will happily help whoever is doing it if it is part of the daily routine. It is also rather unfair to do it all for her until she is, say, five, and then suddenly expect her to start doing it. Anyway, children, like adults, often enjoy the results of making order out of chaos so there's no reason to leave them out.

Many adults don't know about clearing up because somebody else always found it quicker to do it for them; and the results are now to be seen on a global scale. Planet Earth is in a mess because, for centuries, insufficient people have been aware of the consequences of their own actions. However, it would be unhealthy and unnatural for the eager toddler-explorer, keen to get on with her work, to have to stop and think about the mess she might make before she starts, which is what she needs to have learned to do by the time she is an adult. The toddler can't reason this way yet. Better to allow her access to playthings which don't make too grim a mess so that she can help to clear up as a matter of course. While she does so, she will become aware that clearing up is a part of any enterprise, is not a chore tacked on the end but is integral to the process itself.

However, there are children, even as young as two, who may start a game or make a construction that they could go on playing with the next day. If these are always cleared away, the child never achieves the continuity she is seeking. Knowing exactly when to put them away is quite an art, but it is better to leave them out too long than to be forever effectively blocking long-term ideas. If it's going to be in the way, try to get the child to make it on a board that can be moved, or in a corner where it won't be in the way. Most of us have had the experience of having things tidied away by some well-meaning person when we thought we were in the middle of using them. It can be very discouraging, even though we as adults can understand the motives of the tidier-up, which the child does not. If we want him to be creative, having stuff around is the price we pay – or, conversely, the reward we have to live with.

## DIFFERENT LEVELS OF INTERVENTION

The child of toddler age can be, like anybody else, a great trial or utter bliss. She is a great trial if those around her cannot adjust to her without losing sight of their own goals, and quite delightful if they can. Life should not be centred around her. If an adult is busy and the child is not interested in the adult's activity, she can find herself something to do – although she is less inclined to do this if the adult is reading, because she doesn't understand that need. (If the parent wants to read, but is being interrupted the best place to do so is at the sink, if the child isn't helping with the washing-up. You prop the book up behind the taps and keep a dishmop in hand. The child thinks you are actively busy, and will leave you alone.)

As with the literature devoted to infants, much of the child-care literature on toddlers leads parents to worry that their child is not learning or active, and may be 'bored'. Some parents end up becoming almost full-time entertainers. Even Penelope Leach, whose advice to parents can sometimes make them wonder if they will ever do enough for their child, doesn't want parents child-led. She suggests that 'sometimes you play with her for as long as she likes' but her basic message is not that. She goes for minimal intervention. Leach knows how easy and tempting it is to keep trying to make life easier for the toddler. She is also against trying to impose your own play ideas on the child. Leach's platform all through her book is one in which you try to put yourself in the child's place, as when relating to anybody else, while bearing in mind the importance of your own thoughts and actions.

> When she cannot quite do something, lend her your co-ordinated muscles, your height, and your weight, but make sure that you stop when her immediate problem is solved.
> Penelope Leach, *Baby and Child*

Finding the balance between your interests and the child's can be trying, but less so if life can be slowed down a bit. The toddler seems to be either racing around or dawdling, and dawdling conflicts with the modern ethos of speed and productivity with which we are all imbued. If the child wants to stop and look at every tree and every garden gate on the way to the shops, it may be very irritating, but provided you allow enough time to get to the shops, it can be incredibly enlightening. Looking with her at details in the local environment may open your eyes to much that you have never previously had time to notice. For the child such observation is part of the joy of walking anywhere. The walk itself counts, not just the end result. Obviously, if the adult is tired or in a hurry, it makes sense, rather than having an argument all the way, to strap the child into a pushchair or put her into a shoulder carrier and move. And if dawdling on the way to the shops is really irritating, because to you shopping is just shopping, then maybe you can find some other time to dawdle – in the park after lunch, or even in the morning. Many mothers have found great joy in the plants and trees of the park. They have had the time to look that most people simply can't find in the ordinary course of events, or may feel guilty about doing if there's an unread file on their desk, an unwashed car on the street or a meeting for which they should arrive a bit early.

> Don't bustle up with the ping-pong ball and the chalks when she is busily engaged with her bricks. If you do, you are rudely implying that what she is doing is of no importance. You are interrupting her.
>
> Penelope Leach, *Baby and Child*

We can relearn the delights of sloth from our children. Sitting in the wood, fiddling with dead leaves, looking at the light on the trees with them before they move off to investigate something else, is an antidote to stress at least as effective as those we can purchase in the marketplace, in front of the TV, in alcohol, drugs or relaxation classes. It is rare, even in a city, to be unable to find an island of calm somewhere, and to have small children to take there gives us an excuse, if we need one. Self-indulgence has got a bad name, but this type of self-indulgence should not be a cause for guilt; it is one of the rewards of adopting a slower, more peaceful approach to life and childrearing. It can also transform an apparent chore into a treat. I used to get very annoyed when my one-year-old son insisted that I stay in his room after I had told him a story, while he went to sleep, which took about 20 minutes. But when a friend pointed out that it was a perfectly reasonable request, and that I should try to enjoy sitting still on the child's bed, because I probably had no other time during the day for that amount of peace and quiet, my 20 minutes of mild irritation turned into 20 minutes of regeneration. I was rather sad when, before he was two, he decided he didn't want me any more and sent me packing as soon as his story was finished.

## PEACE, QUIET AND TELEVISION

Times of reflection are important both to adults and children. Unfortunately the old-fashioned idea that the child needed a midday nap, or at least a quiet time is not *de rigeur* as it once was (although it does appear in some of the literature). One of the reasons for its disappearance is that there are now sufficient television programmes on, or video tapes available, at suitable times of day for the caretaker to get 'time off' while the child is screenbound. According to the experts, an adult should watch with the child, but that rather defeats the point if the adult wants a break. Some people would argue that relaxing in front of the box is as good as sleep. And it may be for the adult, who is familiar with the kind of images he is going to see and can treat the set as an aid to a daydream. None the less, he is bombarded with the rattling sound. But the child is also being bombarded with a whole lot of extra information to process. (See Chapter 2 on the results of this.)

It is not clear what role, if any, television has to play in the lives of Green toddlers. It is not necessary as a socialising medium since the child is not at an age where discussions with peers of common but absent interests take place, and she is also not yet subject to peer-group pressures as she will be later. There's still a lot of real-life world for her to explore before she needs to start on secondhand experiences. It may be desirable if there is something on which is more worth watching than any alternative activity, and if neither she nor her caretaker can think of anything else to do. It is, however, undesirable for it to be a part of the child's daily routine. Television dependence is a fairly common syndrome, and once the child has adopted the habit of regular viewing, not only is it difficult to break the habit but she may want to watch for longer and longer periods. Some people watch the same programme every day with their children, and find this routine helpful in lending a structure to the day and a rhythm to life. This seems as good a reason as any for habitual daily viewing, although it could be argued that structure and rhythm might be better determined by mealtimes or by the daily walk to feed the ducks.

But sooner or later the television issue has to be faced. If you don't have a set, there is no problem with the toddler. Later in childhood, many children may feel disadvantaged if they don't watch. The obvious compromise for the television-shy adult is to keep the child off it for as long as seems possible. Most habits are harder to break than they are to start (biscuits and sweets would be another example). If she doesn't see you watching, and you don't turn it on, there will be no arguments at this stage. On the other hand, if half-an-hour's television would make the difference between parental sanity and collapse, then it's a useful short-term solution.

## SANITY SAVERS

Sanity can, however, be restored for both parent and child if there is somebody else around. Children like playing around other children, and welcome some changes of scene and face. And once they have got used to other children and their houses, they can be left there so that the caretaker can have some free time. The earlier this system is started, and the more familiar the child is with the non-home situation, the happier she will be when left.

If the adults enjoy each other's company and are not leaving the children, these meetings could be given a purpose. Examples of what people do with toddlers around include sewing groups, language classes, book study groups, cookery sessions, etc., and there are even campaign and consciousness-raising groups. One Friends of the Earth mother and toddler group discusses the issues with which parents are currently concerned, and relates them specifically to the age of their babies. They might be doing some research on products made for babies, or campaigning for local shops to provide environmentally-friendly products related to their needs. Others with toddlers have found it possible to start toy libraries, which are a useful way of cutting down on toy consumption, and others have organised bulk-buy health food co-ops to improve their diet at low cost.

This is all very well for the child whose parents do not both go out to work. Sometimes, a parent is working in order to fulfil himself, rather than because the family needs the money. The activities described above could themselves provide fulfilment (as well as being socially desirable) and thus remove the need for the parent to work. However, some families want or need to have both parents at work; and even though maternity provisions have become more flexible, many mothers are still expected back at work when their child is less than a year old. Some of the ideas in this chapter will then seem rather remote, unless good Green in-house care is available. If fulltime work is not essential, it is often possible to share the children's care with another part-time worker. You may have to accept the fact that your child comes home having lunched on frozen beefburgers and Coca-Cola and watched a cartoon video on the television, but if you are still basically determining the child's lifestyle and you stick to your guns, your child will continue to respect your values. However, having said this, it is important, if you feel strongly about lifestyle, to know what goes on when you are not there. At the latter end of toddlerhood the child will have a sufficient grasp of language to tell you. At the early end she does not. However, she does have sufficient intuition to understand if you disapprove of sweets or television. If she gets these at her minder's, and picks up your disapproval, she may be unhappy and confused. So it is vital that, although you are firm in the assertion of your own values, you do not show disapproval of what happens to her elsewhere. If you are worried, and need to talk about it, the carer can be phoned for a chat, or visited, after the child is in bed. To switch childcare provision because you do not like what the carer does may also be counterproductive. The child may have grown to love her substitute mother, and to feel safe – and whatever you are unhappy about your child eating or doing, what she needs above anything else are love and security.

If you and your partner, if you have one, share similar outlooks on childrearing (which is not always the case) the obvious solution is for both of you to try to shorten your working hours while the children are very young, even if this involves a drop in income or a deferral of promotion. As employment conditions now stand, this possibility is rare, but it's always worth trying as employers can sometimes be budged from even the most entrenched of positions. Or it might be possible for one or both partners to make up for an afternoon's work by doing it at home in the evenings. This is not a soft option, but it doesn't have to go on for ever.

And it is important that boys see males as models of nurture if we want them to develop their own ability to do so. The more a man can be around the house, the better – and not just the man who plays cricket on the lawn on Sunday afternoons (see Chapter 8). I was once in the house of a two-year-old boy who had for some time been looked after principally by his father. I was talking with the father when we heard a loud crash from the bathroom. The father went to investigate. The noise had been a jar falling down from the bathroom shelf as Tommy stood precariously on the loo trying to get down a new roll of loo paper from the shelf to replace the one that had just run out. Many wives would consider it a miracle even for their husbands to do such a task, let alone a child. But it was no miracle, just a boy brought up in the knowledge that men can care too – a competent toddler looking after his environment.

## FURTHER READING

*Happy Children,* Rudolf Dreikurs, Fontana, London, 1972. How to help children learn about the results of their actions without directly teaching them. Maybe he goes a bit far sometimes, but his ideas greatly reduce conflict and self-doubt.

*Toddlers and Parents,* T. Berry Brazelton, Penguin, London, 1979. Commonsense reassurance from a child psychologist. Also sometimes rather hardline: very much oriented to western child-rearing procedures, so needs modifying for Greenness.

*What Do You Really Want for Your Children?,* Dr Wayne W. Dyer, Bantam Books, New York, 1987. A long book, but entirely geared to helping the child, and yourself, lead a positive creative life. A good basis for thought and action.

*Baby and Child,* Penelope Leach, Michael Joseph, London, 1977. Has a good section with ideas for DIY activities with recycled materials.

Also try to buy, or borrow from a library, one of the many books with 'making things' ideas for small children. I am not quoting any specific ones here because they tend to go out of print much more quickly than they deserve. See what there is in the library, though, and write down any ideas you come across that you like; your child will then begin to see the value of the library as a resource, without you having to tell her.

# 5.
# THE IDEAL HOME FOR CHILDREN?

We were presently within doors, and standing in a hall with a floor of marble mosaic and an open timber roof. There were no windows on the side opposite to the river, but arches below leading into chambers, one of which showed a glimpse of a garden beyond, and above them a long space of wall gaily painted (in fresco, I thought) with similar subjects to those of the frieze outside; everything about the place was handsome and generously solid as to material; and though it was not very large (somewhat smaller than Crosby Hall perhaps), one felt in it that exhilarating sense of space and freedom which satisfactory architecture always gives to an unanxious man who is in the habit of using his eyes.

*News from Nowhere*, William Morris

The passage in the box is taken from Morris's vision of Utopia, which he wrote as a reaction to the squalor of 19th-century industrialisation and its negative effect on the human spirit. Although his book is seldom read now, we have appropriated from his work what we felt we needed – his design ideas and patterns. Morris felt beautiful but simple surroundings, and timeless and straightforward designs whose inspiration came from nature, helped people to lead lives both happy and noble.

It is possibly as a reaction to industrial design and the dreariness of much modern architecture that the restoration of old and neglected houses by the middle-classes has become almost a national pastime. The results are often very splendid, since the utmost care is taken by the house owners and little expense is spared. However, there is every reason to suppose that these 'permanent' restorations are actually only temporary, given the efforts of home fashion makers to keep us dissatisfied by producing ever new possible 'improvements'.

> Twenty, or was it thirty, years ago, I boxed in all their stairs and took out their fireplaces. Fifteen years ago I painted all their woodwork white. Now I go in and strip all the paint off their doors and nice painted dressers, and put their fireplaces back, or somebody's fancy fireplace. I don't know what I'll be doing ten years on, but it's all good for business.
>
> South London builder

The results of the builder's work described in the box above are very pleasant, and the structural fabric of many houses improved by him or others has been repaired in a way that should, theoretically, greatly prolong their lives. Unfortunately, since there is a shortage of skilled craftsmen, and because many houseowners are in a hurry, much of the improvement work has been done quickly and cheaply, using materials whose long-term toxic effects may be very serious and many of which are not yet known. Chemically treated wood is one of these; others include paint strippers, huge quantities of glue, and chipboard bound with formaldehyde.

These restored houses often look beautiful, and frequently bear an uncanny resemblance to illustrations from *Homes and Gardens* or from the lifestyle sections of colour supplements. But they are a far cry from what Morris envisaged; simple, uncluttered homes in which simple and convivial lives could be led. He had apparently not foreseen that apparently simple houses might be filled up with complicated and energy-consuming gadgetry and become barely used bases for complicated lives. Nor did he foresee the isolated castles such houses could become, being private childrearing centres, private laundries, private entertainment complexes, inhabited by people who are encouraged to put their private gratifications before the well-being of the community. Members of his Utopia would have kept their doors fearlessly open on to a street which they would have made sure was as pleasant as their house. Sadly, it hasn't worked out like that.

## THE REAL COSTS OF HOME IMPROVEMENT

A row of Edwardian terraced houses stretches away down the hill. Outside two of the houses there are skips, in one of which a perfectly good kitchen cabinet has been ruined by rain. From the other, dust containing heaven knows what is blowing across the street.

The kitchen cabinet, in the process of being destroyed, is more than a piece of furniture. It is also a symbol of the near-obsession with perfecting the home environment that has been created by manufacturers and sold through the usual media channels. The skip is an eyesore which has been there for weeks, and is itself a symbol of wholesale waste. There's a lot of rubble round it, and the pavement is covered in cement from the building works. It is never adequately cleaned up and will deface the pavement permanently.

As you will have guessed, somebody is 'having the house done up'. Nobody is living there yet. They will probably move in before the alterations are complete, and then many of their thoughts and conversations will be directed towards the awfulness of living with builders in the house. Friends will reassure them about how lovely it will be when it is finished, and how lucky they were to buy their home so cheaply. A few years later these friends will comment idly 'I wonder what it's worth now?' A house has almost ceased to be a home; its price is considered as valid a topic of conversation as its history.

Nobody looks out at the skip and asks what its contents are worth. Our distorted economics-based definitions of cost exclude the fact that what each individual throws away constitutes a cost to society. It may be something that would have been of use to somebody else, or, if it is beyond use, there is a cost involved in disposing of it; many acres of land are now used as rubbish tips, and are generating undesirable side effects in the atmosphere and the soil. The new owners of the house could have had a garage sale, making the old stuff available to others, but it did not seem worth their while to make that sort of effort for a couple of hundred pounds when the replacements were to cost tens of thousands. It was easier to junk the lot. And anyway, their friends might have considered them rather odd if they had spent a couple of Saturdays running such a sale.

Instead the Saturdays were spent trailing round the shops looking for exactly the right kind of furniture with their children who will grow up considering such activity perfectly normal (a recent survey indicated that the British spend on average one-fifth of their waking hours shopping). The Saturdays were no fun because they could never find exactly what they thought they wanted, and though what they could afford was pleasant and functional, what they would ideally have chosen was just beyond the reach of their credit cards. However, they knew the day might come when they could afford it – depending on what happened to the enormous mortgage they had had to take on to fund their 'improvements'.

In a crowded urban world, we need a private space in which we can get away from the crowd and feel entirely ourselves. But there are always several ways of reaching a given target, and the cost to society of the creation of private spaces could be significantly reduced if advertisers were not exerting so much pressure and if more imaginative, environmentally-friendly and less wasteful solutions were socially acceptable.

Home means different things to different people. Margaret, who lives at the bottom of the roadful of skips, has another view. She and her husband bought a house ten years previously in a similar condition. Since another family had been living in it when they arrived they assumed that it must be habitable. There were two or three structural faults, which they remedied; apart from that all they did immediately was to put a couple of coats of paint over such of the decor as they found too garish for their tastes. They managed to resist the call of huge mortgages and credit cards, preferring to make gradual alterations. They wanted to get the feel of the house, and in any case they had a family and did not want to neglect them for the sake of a house, or to have to work long hours to pay builders' bills. They talked about their home rather than their house, and provided a welcome for stray callers and meetings for local groups to which they belonged, as well as their children's friends. These friends not only liked the easy atmosphere, but were overjoyed to be able, on occasions, to join in the painting of real emulsion on real walls. All that most of them knew about walls was that they would get into trouble if walls got dirty. Even in their own bedrooms, which were theoretically their own spaces, they were not free to do as they chose.

The ideal home of today, as well as being environmentally damaging, is not really suitable for children. It is a prime example of really expensive wants and a really powerful message being created by producers, reinforced by magazines, television images and chains of DIY stores – although sometimes, in the less glossy magazines, a refreshing article appears about how to use a saw and a pot of paint to transform an ugly article, or how to recover an apparently dead sofa with an old pair of curtains, activities in which most children can lend a helping hand. But mending, one of the most important skills we can model for our children, is not normally a central part of the message.

Instead the message given by the home improvement cult is about revolutionary rather than evolutionary change, about the compulsive replacement of old by new rather than processes of adaptation. The revolution leads to the age of perfection, with fitted kitchens and glamour reflecting uniformity, efficiency, sterility and luxury. Panels of switches, pale plastic labour-saving gadgets and white tiled floors must be kept clean, and half-empty coffee jars, minor spills or dirty washing-up left on the draining board destroy the image. Too many signs of imperfect life are not at home on glass-topped tables, or in an environment dominated by rows of hungry white machines defining the prodigal way our lives are led.

## LABOUR-SAVING DEVICES AND OUR KIDS

The dishwasher, one of the hungriest white machines, is a prime example of a grossly unecological solution for the private home, and one whose presence deprives visitors and children of the privilege and dignity of helping to contribute to the running of the home. An 'economical' dishwasher uses about 30 litres of water per wash, heated to a very high temperature. If its owner is well organised, fills it during the day and only switches it on at night, he does not need a great deal of crockery. If not, he has to have enough to use while one lot waits in the machine, with old food drying on plates so that only extremely hot water and a long wash will clean the dishes. It cannot scrub saucepans, so there is always a residue of washing-up that must be done by hand. It makes a lot of noise, and it is yet another source of electrical pollution. (This is a problem currently being researched since evidence began to surface that electrical appliances, because of the frequencies they emit, may themselves be a source of fatigue and other minor forms of ill-health.)

The intermediate technology solution to washing-up is a double sink and a draining rack (more hygienic than a tea towel, and the crockery can live on it). Using about 6 litres of hot water for each wash – 18 litres in a day – and washing up before the food scraps have hardened is far less wasteful of resources, will not need the help of a machine repairer or the use of all the special powders and solvents that are needed by the machine, can be a social event, need take no more than a few minutes, and reduces the home's fuel bills and global overconsumption of energy. It also accustoms children to the idea of clearing up as a pleasant, integrated part of the mealtime ritual.

Many people claim that dishwashers are economic, and that their lives have been transformed by them. But as usual, there is more than one way to transform lives. If there is no dishwasher, it is possible, with a certain amount of forethought, to generate less washing-up – and the generation of less side effects is central to Green philosophy and practice.

The tumble-drier, another huge consumer of electricity, is another case of a machine creating its own input. Because it is permanently there in the corner, like the washing machine, more clothes can be washed and dried far more randomly than they could before. Like many labour-saving devices, it is a stimulus to disorganisation, and it reduces the life of the clothes fed to it (think how much fluff – in reality bits of clothing – have to be cleaned out of the filter). Many modern children do not know that clothes will dry themselves on a washing line or a clothes horse, without electrical help; our own dependence on these machines, which we know are not strictly necessary, leads children to think that they are necessary. They have no other experience – as I found out when our washing machine broke down and my own five-year old asked how 'clothes would be got clean if the machine was not working'.

The modern kitchen, equipped with such machines, has become a model of mass production and industrial efficiency within the home. Although many modern kitchens are dressed up to look like 'farmhouse' kitchens, with pine units and quarry-tiled floors, their appearance is deceptive. The 'farmhouse' kitchen is, in many respects, the heart of the family, the major source of its physical and emotional well-being and growth. Symbolically, it is rather like the breast to which the tired or distressed baby returns for comfort. Indeed, the smell of bread baking in a kitchen must still speak to our hearts, because one estate agent suggested that to have bread baking when you were showing a house to prospective buyers would increase the chances of making a sale – the smell made the house feel like a home!

To allow a child to contribute in the kitchen, as and when he is able, is to allow him access to the control room of nurture. But he cannot have such access if all vegetables are chopped in dangerous machines, if all washing-up and washing is done at the touch of a button, if most of the appliances are too fragile, hazardous and complicated for him to be allowed to use. He must go into the next room and watch a video while someone else does an 'efficient' job of preparing the food.

As a result of the scares associated with food poisoning from instant TV dinners, there has been a comment in the media lately about the apparently decreasing ability of people to cook 'real' food. It would appear that food preparation is no longer a known basic skill, because we have been sold the virtues of part-prepared or entirely pre-prepared foods for so long, and children have been out of the kitchen at meal preparation (or re-heating?) time. Experience and methods were once handed down in families, although often only to girls, but this is no longer common. The prospect of meal preparation has therefore become daunting, because the instinctiveness and speed with which our grandmothers did it, which made it less of a conscious effort, depend on practice and habit.

The child who knows about the preparation of good food, and who is involved from an early stage, will be a freer adult than the one who does not. He is freer because he can chose what he eats; because he will know about economy and the re-use of foods he will not be tied to earning a large income. And if he can use a knife, a board, a bowl and a wooden spoon, he will be freed from having to get involved with a bevy of machines which will invite him to consume resources and will complicate his life.

From the parents' point of view, there's a lot to be gained from a Green approach, minimising dependence on high technology and encouraging every member of the family to join in the nurturing. Children love to cook and, if they can handle a simple kitchen, will be able to do their share unaided by the time they are about eight, and sometimes younger (a competent five-year-old can turn out a decent fruit salad). If they have worked alongside a systematic adult they will not make a ghastly mess. Their joy in cooking, once they have learnt a few basic skills and recipes, often leads to the production of dishes which adults would never have thought of. And it's reassuring to a parent to know that if he is ill, he can stay in bed and the children won't starve.

## GUILT AND THE IDEAL HOME

The rest of the house matters, although perhaps not so fundamentally. Most of us want to make it pleasant and keep it reasonably ordered, and there is every reason to do so. But excessive striving to glamorise our abodes and reflect currently fashionable tastes produces worry for ourselves and a source of guilt for our children. The worry is keeping it nice – as one mother ruefully told me, you can't pull the pram in from a wet pavement on to a pale pink carpet. And it makes extra work for ourselves, because the more perfect the house, the more it drives its owner to hoovering and the use of (mostly harmful) cleaning chemicals, particularly if there are children about making a mess.

We do not need houses which make anybody feel worried, or guilty. But children can easily get in this state if they spoil what is beautiful. If they see their parents labouring for hours to perfect their home and they then accidentally spoil it, they can feel very bad at having let their parents down. Actually, if they have been allowed to join in the decorating and to help choose what goes into the home, they are both more likely to be careful and less likely to feel guilty, because any damage is damage to their own work as much as to anybody else's. And the minimisation of guilt in the child is fundamental to the enhancement of the child's self-esteem.

It can be beneficial to have one room which looks lovely and which is always fit for special occasions (it used to be called the front room or parlour, even in very small houses, and was lovingly always kept ready for 'best'). Even if it is unrealistic to expect small children to be very careful all the time, it is perfectly reasonable to expect them to be careful in short bursts as, for example, on those occasions when they are allowed into the front room. The pale pink carpet would then be at home in this room, as it might in the rest of the house when the children are older. But the carpet which reduces stress and guilt for the rest of the house is less beautiful; it could be secondhand or come off a skip, or, indeed, be replaced by easy-wipe lino or cork.

Although such solutions are cheap and liberating from cares, they are not publicised because they do not sell goods; it can even be difficult to admit that you use such solutions. One mother asked me to look after her children for a few hours as there was 'something she wanted to do'. When she came to collect them, I said I hoped she had had enough time to do whatever it was – I was actually rather curious about her secrecy. In tones of great shame she said they had been given some fire-damaged carpet which could be cut to fit their room, and that they had just been fitting it. But she said she hadn't been going to say what she was doing because she felt bad about getting carpet secondhand and free, 'when it was really very nice'. What she deserved was a medal, not guilty feelings. To feel guilty about recycling used material, making good use of old resources to improve a home, is ridiculous and can only happen in a culture in which we are persuaded to believe that large sums of money need to be spent if we are to do justice to the home our family deserves.

## AND GARDEN BEAUTIFUL

The kind of transformation symbolised by the cabinet on the skip, with instant effect valued over gradual alteration, has now been moved out into the garden. A junior school teacher described how garden centre gardening had undermined his attempts to demonstrate growth. He was growing fruit trees from pips, and they were taking a long time. One Monday morning one of his class came in and said 'You don't need to grow apple trees from pips, you could go and buy them at the garden centre.' Evidently he and his parents had had an expedition there on Sunday, and had bought enough shrubs and trees to populate a botanical garden. They had also bought several massive bags of peat, dug up from rapidly-depleting peat bogs, in which to plant shrubs for which their own soil was unsuitable, rather than selecting the plants which would be at home with their existing type of soil. (There are now over 30,000 types of garden plant to choose from, so a choice of appropriate plant is always possible, although it may have to be bought by post from a specialist nursery if it is not one of the more popular varieties.)

Apart from the unsuitable shrubs, it is obviously a good thing to plant trees, even intensively and artificially reared ones. Yet for a child it is exciting to see the results of slow growth that he has instigated. The pride of a child who finally plants out an apple tree that he grew from a pip planted three years previously, or a cutting from someone else's garden that he has nursed for 18 months, is a pride that itself needs cultivating. If you have a garden, it is an ideal place for a child to learn about nurturing. As with houses, compromise may be the only way we can both satisfy our adult need for immediate results with the need to help the child to nurture and to contribute; we may have to sacrifice some of our own ideas about what the garden should look like in order to accommodate opportunities for the child. We may not, for example, like 'children's flower mixture' but if we allow our children to sow some of these seeds in the garden, they will really see results. They can plant bulbs, which have a higher success rate than seeds. They can weed. They can dig. They can deadhead plants. And they do like to be allowed to help choose what is grown. If they can have a small patch of their own and be allowed a free hand, they will learn a great deal, especially if adults refrain from helping them out.

Another reason for compromising our own ideas is when friends offer us plants from their gardens. They may not fit the colour scheme you had in mind, but often, if you accept these, the commercial garden centre can be avoided altogether. Not only is this cheap but it also populates the gardens with memories and symbols of friendship – helenium from Mary, lilies-of-the-valley from Granny, rosemary from Robin, feverfew from William. To have a tree in your garden grown from two leaves of a loved ex-neighbour's tree is to have taken something of the neighbour with you. In the garden, compromising over choice of plant is only one example of the need to allow ourselves to fall short of perfection if we are to remain sane. Many of us have battled to keep a lawn perfect, for example, but it is almost impossible to do so without constant vigilance because it is ecologically maladapted. It is an unnatural monoculture and is happier with some weeds in it. (Perhaps we can also allow our children a few of what we choose to call weeds if they particularly like the flowers or leaves, and if they aren't horrendously invasive, by just leaving them to grow where they are.)

We could reject all the fashionable notions of smart town gardens and go for an ecological garden. We can plant vegetables among the flowers; we can plant so that the system in our garden is more or less self-sustaining; and even in the middle of a busy city we can plant (or grow) species that will encourage specific forms of wildlife, such as birds or butterflies (see Chapter 13 for details). We can let some of even the smallest garden become slightly overgrown; make a pond by sinking a washing-up bowl into the soil and put some tadpoles in it. Then we can go out and enjoy the worms and woodlice with our children. We can dig the soil with them, and make our own compost, returning to the soil that which came from it. And we can leave some of our fallen leaves unraked, and the following year watch with our children the spring shoots appearing among the leaf skeletons. In doing all this, we give ourselves a chance to recapture some of our sense of the wonder of nature with our children.

If you have no garden, window boxes and indoor gardening can provide many similar opportunities (see Chapter 13). Or you might like to rent an allotment near you. Here you and the children will have the space to grow appreciable quantities of vegetables, as well as flowers. Children are always pleased to be able to pick vegetables they have grown to feed their family (and others). In cultivating an allotment, not only are you growing for yourselves but you are sustaining a piece of public land, connecting your family's nurturing to a wider world. Gardening on an allotment is an experience like no other.

For the town-dweller the allotment provides a country afternoon out with a purpose, a breathing space and a creative alternative to endless dreary car rides to escape to an outdoor environment. It extends the possibilities of DIY near home and of constructive contributions by children far beyond those inherent in building yet another storage unit to house ever more household clutter. As an extension to the household, it takes us out rather than shutting us in determinedly in our own private palace, which is what the ideal home culture would like to persuade us to do. And, above all else, it teaches us to love our weather, to work with it and to realise its importance. The child who has tried to work a garden or allotment in a drought can really begin to understand for himself what water, the principal component of most living things, really means, and why it should not be taken for granted.

The allotment landscape is a rich one and, despite the easy jibes, has inspired artists like Harry Allen and Edward Burra, and the Royal Academy summer exhibition frequently carries an allotment painting, or etching. The allotment represents communal activity amongst people with a real stake in the land. It represents an escape from the competitive social relations and commercialisation of our culture; its land and landscape, unlike the bulk of contemporary Britain, is not a commodity. People work together, sharing ideas and experiences; swap materials and seeds; argue with the landowner in defence of their rights, help each other create buildings, however short of the precise standards of our material culture.

It is this combination of creative alternative and release that for decades has routed predictions from the 'informed' that the allotment, tainted with the image of ration books, was on its way out ... the attraction, the meaning of cultivation, and cultural participation on the allotment is significant because it is so deep.

The allotment is a peopled landscape, not the empty one that we so frequently see and are 'sold'. It contains a depth of communal and co-operative relationship that provides a deeper value of experience, through those whose efforts relate in the ground they make, an expression of humanity.
David Crouch, 'The Allotment: A Culture and Landscape', extract from *Quaker Monthly*, May 1989

## FURTHER READING

*Home Ecology, Making Your World a Better Place*, Karen Christensen, Arlington, London, 1989. Straightforward advice on how individuals can contribute to protecting the environment and reduce the stresses of modern urban and suburban life. Covers all aspects of daily life and how to Green them.

*The Green Consumer Guide*, John Elkington and Julia Hailes, Gollancz, London, 1988. A bit of a red herring – more about minor modifications than serious change. Useful on toxicity, etc.

*The Pauper's Home-Making Book*, Jocasta Innes, Penguin, London, 1976. Not strictly speaking Green, and it would be worth checking on the toxicity of some of the materials she recommends. But crammed with good ideas about how to make much from little.

*Green Pages – A Directory of Natural Products, Services, Resources and Ideas*, compiled by John Button, Macdonald Optima, London, 1988.

*The Allotment Book*, Gillie Gould and Rob Bullock, Macdonald Optima, London, 1988. All you need to know, with emphasis on organic methods.

*The Allotment: A Culture and Landscape*, David Crouch and Colin Ward, Faber & Faber, London, 1988.

For gardening, almost everything you need to know or buy can be obtained from the Henry Doubleday Research Association, National Centre for Organic Gardening, Ryton-on-Dunsmore, Coventry CV8 3LG, 0203 303517. Do write to them.

On homes, information can be obtained from the Women's Environmental Network, 287 City Road, London EC1V 1LA.

# 6.
# FROM TODDLERHOOD TO SCHOOL

'We're going for a walk. Please could you put on your coat and shoes.' By the time he is about two-and-a-half, he can, and might do willingly if he wants to go. But whether he is able to both find his coat and then put it on depends on whether his home is organised so that he is in control of this. If the coat is hung on a high peg and has a complicated zip, he is adult-dependent and cannot look after himself.

The more the child is able to use his increased abilities, the higher his self-respect will be and the lower will be the number of daily chores that have to be performed for him. The time spent in observing what he can now do, and making sure it is possible, really pays off, particularly if there is another child around needing more attention. However, he will not yet be consistent in always doing what he actually can do, for he still needs care and attention. Even if he can do up his own shoes, sometimes he will and sometimes he won't.

He likes to decide what to wear and to dress himself, and this is a choice he can be allowed to make. It may be embarrassing to take out a child who has put his vest on over his T-shirt, but it is irrational and patronising to insist that he be re-dressed when he has achieved this by himself. His peers won't notice or mind. It may be that other mothers look askance at him, but they'll be polite enough not to comment in front of him and you will know that your child is choosing for, and doing for, himself.

His life, and yours, will be easier if you can acquire clothes without fastenings. Elasticated trousers, skirts and T-shirts can be managed by him, and maybe even a few buttons if they are big enough. Small buttons, back fastenings and slide-in zips are to be avoided, as are shoelaces. Similarly he can handle much of his own toileting procedure if he can reach the lavatory and basin. If he can't, an old scrap of wood with legs firmly screwed on makes a useful platform, particularly for a boy when he wants to stand up to use the loo.

His language is becoming quite sophisticated by now and he understands what he may or may not do, and may ask if he is unsure. If he is used to reason, he is less likely to be rebellious now than if he has only ever been bossed about. He is like an adult in this respect; most of us will do something more willingly for someone we consider reasonable than someone we have discovered is not. He does not understand long-winded explanations about why he has to do something, but 'If we go shopping now, we'll be home when Dad gets in from work' will make some sense to him, even if it is only the tone in which it is said.

For he wants to cooperate most of the time. His increased cooperation enables him to play with friends for extended periods without constant supervision, unless he lives in a house beautiful or dangerous, whose beauty may be hard to sustain during this highly experimental phase. Sand and water are fascinating to him, but messy; playdough is enormous fun to press through the garlic press; paste and paper have endless possibilities; but none of these playthings is pristine-house friendly.

At this age his self-esteem can be boosted by the making of an 'I can' book. He may not need it, but it can be introduced at any stage if the child appears to be feeling inadequate. This is a looseleaf or scrapbook, and into it go, for example, a picture by the child or parent of a model the child has made. At the top of each page the parent (with the child's help?) writes in large letters 'I CAN'. Underneath each picture she writes (or he does, when he can write) 'make a house', 'draw a boat', 'reach the breakfast bar', 'swing on the bottom bar of the climbing frame', 'make fruit salad', 'stir a cake', or whatever he has just done. It's a bit like a diary, only there's no real need to date it, and it is useful as a reminder to a self-doubting child of all the things he can do. It can be kept up for years, if wanted or needed, and started and stopped at any time.

## DIY PLAYTHINGS

If you do not already have one, it is helpful to have a table at which he can work or a large PVC cloth to put over a good table. His own table can be made quite cheaply if you shorten the legs of a junk shop kitchen table. A couple of folding fishing stools, for a couple of pounds each, complete his work furniture, which does not separate him from adults into an expensive world of garish, unbiodegradable, moulded plastic. His table can be painted in a colour of his choice, if needed, and then he has a highly personalised suite that speaks of more care and thought than any number of plastic chairs with Disneyland faces on them. He can always stick stickers on them, too (perhaps Disney ones?). His involvement with the creation of his own furniture also gives him the knowledge that he has the power to change it. A play-tray is also useful – just an ordinary tray with rims at the side and a wipeable surface, as large as you can make or find. He can start a puzzle on this, or some modelling, and then the tray can be moved out of the way when needed. If he's stuck in bed he can use it for painting.

Painting is popular with this age group. Most of the painting kits sold in the shops are unsuitable. Thick paints and stubby brushes are the answer, and if you buy large quantities of a few colours, plus black and white, other colours can be mixed. Powder paint is the cheapest, but poster paint is the easiest texture to use, keeps for years, and can be thinned. Expensive paper is not necessary, as at this age the child is more interested in process than product – he can even paint on newspaper. If you can get hold of a pile of used computer paper this is particularly useful, because the sheets are large and they can be torn off one at a time or used together. One pile 50 cm thick will last for literally years.

He can combine painting with sticking. Not only is it jolly useful to have a collection of old Christmas cards and magazine pictures available, but leaves, twigs, bits of spaghetti, etc., can be made available to him (pressed leaves make very pretty pictures). If he sees you making your own cards out of pressed leaves and petals, or pasting up old ones with a label inside for re-use, he will want to do it with you. When Christmas comes you will find you don't have to buy a single card.

## PRESSURES ON PRESCHOOLERS

The pressure to 'educate' the child, and to 'socialise' him intensifies at this stage. The current doctrine is that the child needs preschool education. All kinds of reasons are given for this 'need'. Firstly, he 'needs' more than his home can offer him, in terms of stimuli and play materials. Secondly, he 'needs' the company of other children. Thirdly, his adaptation to school will be easier if he has been to preschool than if he has not.

All these statements are open to question. Whether or not the childs needs more than his home can offer is entirely dependent on him and his home. There are many parents, indeed, who feel that the quiet concentration of home and what is on offer there is quite sufficient for the child. And research makes it clear that language is certainly much better learnt one to one, such as at home, than in a larger institution.

His 'need' for other children may or may not exist. If it does, whether it has to be met by any kind of institution will depend on how much contact he has with other children in the general run of his life. If he has brothers and sisters, or friends with whom he regularly plays, he may have enough of other children. If he is in the kind of community in which children of different ages regularly play together, this may actually be better than an age-stratified pre-school group for, as childhood progresses, children get stuck with their immediate peers more and more and the opportunities for valuable exchanges with children both older and younger diminish.

There is some evidence that his adaptation to school is easier if he has been to preschool. Translated, this means that he has been taught to conform to institutional norms earlier. But since many of our institutional and social norms are radically at odds with Green philosophy, is this easy adaptation actually a good thing? He will probably adapt to school eventually in any case. And if he goes to a playgroup or nursery, much of what he has learnt about taking responsibility for himself will be rejected. Teachers and playgroup leaders, while they try to foster a sense of responsibility in their charges, have to look after a heterogeneous group, some members of which may only just be meeting the notion that they are capable of taking some responsibility for themselves when they arrive at the playgroup or nursery. A child who is used to being around when decisions are made and sometimes contributes will not understand, at three, why he is suddenly being treated as incompetent again, and may resent it. The older he is, the more likely he is to understand. He will have to learn about silent acceptance of authority at some stage, but it is better that he should understand the need than resent it, for then he is less likely to think authority exists for its own sake. He will see the need for order.

Unfortunately, the pressure is on to send them to preschool. I personally came under this pressure when my own three-year-old son did not want to go to playgroup like all the other children did. We tried, but he didn't like it. Several people said he obviously needed to learn to get on with other children (which wasn't true, as he had several friends) and helpfully suggested we take him to the playgroup, leave him there and he'd soon 'get used to it'. As he was extremely happy just pottering about his home, and no trouble to anyone, it seemed rather a silly insistence. But we were quite surprised at the extent to which we began to feel like failures. There must be something wrong with us and our child if he couldn't fit in. But we left it, tried again when he was four, at which time he decided he liked it and settled in with no trouble at all.

The opposite can also happen. At about the same time, another mother was rebuked by a playgroup leader because her three-year-old son was going to another playgroup on some afternoons. The leader said it was 'too much' for a three-year-old – even though the child was evidently very happy at both groups and at home. The mother was very worried, but eventually left him there; several other mothers in the same boat did what they were told.

Parents can become quite distressed if their child fails to conform, and can expend enormous amounts of energy persuading him to do so. If next door's two-year-old can be left with anybody, what's wrong with my four-year-old who won't even stay with Granny? And so on. The pressure for standard behaviour and socialisation patterns, and the requirement that children adapt quickly to institutions are offshoots of the general cultural pressure to reach certain norms by a certain time. Sometimes it is social skills, sometimes it is learning. And with regard to learning, we are in a chicken-and-egg situation in which the pressure to achieve has produced many commercial aids, and the existence of these aids has further fuelled the fear that your own child may fail, or that he needs some kind of 'head start'. It is certainly true that many children in unfortunate circumstances do benefit socially and intellectually from specially designed environments, materials and trained staff. It is also true that if a child starts to learn the violin at two he will probably play it better than his peers when he is eight or nine. But by the time he is 14 he may well find that more self-motivated children who started at seven are well ahead of him.

The same could be said of ballet, swimming, reading, writing, almost anything you care to name. Seven is often the best time to start. There are many who were brought up to excel early at such activities and who have later felt that they missed out on a great deal of life, and who have no ability whatsoever to relax and 'play'. It is almost as if the reality of their existence depends upon continuous demonstrable achievements.

There have been some interesting experiments, notably in America, concerned with the acceleration of the intellectual development of small children. So far, they have been successful in speeding it up, but it is not yet known what the long-term results of these experiments will be. They do, however, have some ideas which can usefully be applied by ordinary people in diluted form. For example, they stress the need for exercise as an aid to mental development, and have devised special daily exercise routines. (The Romans and the Greeks, thousands of years ago, had the same idea.) Which gives us another excuse, if we needed one, to enjoy ourselves digging, swimming and going for walks. And rather than worry about specific exercises, the American theory can be translated into the simplicity of going down to the local playground and letting the children swing on the climbing frame, or climbing trees in the park, or playing outdoors with that simplest of toys – a ball.

## CREATIVE TOYS AND PLAYTHINGS

More fuel for parents' fears, and a further distraction from the notion of pure enjoyment, is provided by the name of a newish chain of shops called the Early Learning Centre. Should adult bookshops, or sports shops, by the same reasoning be called Later Learning Centres? There are, as it happens, some good buys there. And it's well worth having a look round for ideas of toys and playthings you might make at home, and possibly improve on. If you measure up some bricks, you may find Grandpa would enjoy making some. Have a look at a hobby-horse. This is a shortened broom handle with a head. You can very easily either make a head yourself from old material, or use an old sock, which is horse-head shaped, as a base and add eyes, mane, bridle, etc. Doing it this way means that the children can easily make their own copies if they wish to run their own stable.

Road layouts can be bought which have streets, trees, buildings, etc., printed on them. Lots of children like vrooming cars about. But it's much more fun to make your own road layout out of cardboard, which you can design as you want, to which you can add new turnings as required, and which can be varied so, for example, it goes on a plank up a 'hill' made by leaning the plank against a step. The cars can then race down this hill. Trees, houses, shops, etc., can be made of twigs, leaves, paper, boxes, and moved around when the child wants a different street or town layout. (Before you make all these bits and pieces, make sure you've got a big enough box to put them in. There's nothing worse than trying to play a game when there are bits missing, and a lot of clutter is equally unsettling.) Incidentally, while cars are being used, another game that is fun is 'Which am I?' You need about five ordinary Matchbox-type cars and a hard floor. First you shoot them across the floor and listen carefully to the different sound made by each one. Then you shut your eyes and take it in turns to vroom them to each other. The game is to spot by ear which car is being vroomed.

Toys like the home-made hobby horse and road system give the child the opportunity to use his imagination both in the making and the playing of the games. He also has the opportunity to expand beyond prescribed commercial limits – his own thinking is what counts. The shop-bought road mat is fixed and irrevocable; it cannot be altered or changed. It may look glossy and professional to the adult eye, but it gives neither parent nor child any scope for their own real control. They are being discouraged from thinking laterally and creatively, and encouraged to accept the vision that somebody else wanted to sell.

Another great standby is the dressing-up box. Rather unlikely garments from your wardrobe, a jumble sale or the Oxfam shop will start this off. It is not necessary to sew a lot of fancy costumes laboriously (although like me, you may enjoy doing this – I've got a passion for turning net curtains into fairies) because children will invent their own combinations. Nor is it necessary to buy any. Hats, bags and other props are useful. Groups of children will invent all kinds of plays and stories based on these old bits and pieces of cloth, and if they need new props for their story, these can easily be made of cardboard. At this age they will, if not spoiled by excessive plastic realism, see what they want to see in an approximate shape. Something more or less oval does for an egg in Jack and the beanstalk, something more-or-less L-shaped for a gun for cowboys.

Plasticine can be used for small, semi-permanent props, and playdough, which can be baked hard and painted, used for more permanent items such as pretend food. There is almost no prop that cannot be made in a few minutes with cardboard, playdough, sticks and stones. You may not 'see it', but they will.

For children, there are a lot of kits available. Some of these kits are useful in getting the child interested in doing or making, and some techniques can be learned from them. But often they are extremely unsuitable, for example knitting kits with small needles and thin wool at a great price – a pair of great fat needles and old thick wool is far more suitable. The same applies to sewing kits. Sewing is best started with a rug needle and a piece of cardboard with holes punched in it. Kits cost money and can provide great frustration, so look at them, see how they could be improved, and do it yourself, better, for a fraction of the cost and half the frustration for the child.

Most playgroups and nurseries have some interesting materials, and it is worth spending some time there to see what they use and how. The novelty of the materials will not wear off just because they have them both at home and playgroup if, like playdough, they are materials with very wide scope. The novelty of very specific toys will wear off, though, because there is a limit to the number of times a child wants to make the same Jack pop out of the same box. But every time he uses paint, playdough, bricks, sand, water, or a ball, the materials will behave differently.

## THE DEVELOPMENT OF LATERAL THINKING

Seeing multiple purposes for items, seeing alternative solutions to problems, making connections in several directions, all are a way of thinking known as lateral thinking, and are characteristics of green philosophies and outlooks. Some people have an instinct for this way of thinking – especially children – while others find it more difficult, for reasons both of nature and nurture. Both lateral and convergent thinking have their place in problem solving, but the importance of lateral thinking has only recently begun to be accepted. Wholistic approaches involve both types of thought. This can be seen from the difference between a 'straight' and an alternative doctor; the ordinary doctor is trained to provide a cure for a specific symptom or set of symptoms, whereas the alternative practitioner is more likely

to view the patient from several angles and follow up the possibility of several approaches to a solution. If you take a simple
home example, say of an electric kettle breaking down, the
convergent thinker is likely to think in terms of repair or
replacement, whereas the lateral thinker is more likely also to
think of ways in which he could do without it altogether. If there
were no milk in the house, a cocoa drink could, for example, be
made with thinned mashed potato by the lateral thinker, while
the convergent thinker might go without or drive around trying
to find some milk. Lateral thinking provides a considerable
amount of mental freedom and freedom from constraints, which
is why its development in the Green child is important. (Junk
art is a great developer of lateral thinking.) Not only is there
often more than one use for any object, but there are at least two
ways of solving every problem.

The importance of the development of lateral thinking cannot
be overstressed if we are to be able to find Green solutions to the
global problem. We need people who can see other alternatives
to the traffic problem apart from building motorways. We need
people who can think of multiple uses for objects so that they
can be recycled and resources saved from the manufacture of an
alternative object. We need people who can think what to do
with themselves when their electricity is rationed. In short, we
need people who can imagine an existence other than the one we
are now being asked to accept.

It is, of course, in the interests of industrial society to make us
forget these possibilities. A tool is made, and sold, that is specific
to each and every conceivable purpose (and sometimes one
wonders whether the purposes were invented in order to sell the
tool). Very precise accessories are needed, for example, to go
with a microwave oven or dishwasher. There is a 'correct'
cleaning agent for every kind of surface – and so on. (Many of
these claims about the correctness of the accessory or cleaning
agent are not true: alternatives can be found.)

## PEER GROUP PRESSURES AND HOW TO DEAL WITH
## ALTERNATIVE VALUES

At playgroup or nursery the child, for the first time in his life,
will be exposed to other children who have not been chosen as
companions by his parents. Which is splendid for the child.
However, if a three-and-a-half year old who has been blissfully

happy with a few old boxes and 20 minutes TV a day becomes a great pal of somebody whose room is stuffed with mechanical toys, who has unlimited access to a video and who appears to eat nothing but sweets, the wails will undoubtedly begin. If you really believe you are right – know you are right – and if you enjoy all the things you are doing with your child, and are including him in your life, just listening to his complaints as you go home from his friend's house (where he has spent the afternoon comatose in front of the 'Incredible Hulk' on TV) will probably suffice to dispel them. You have no right to disapprove of his friend's parents' choices, but you do have the right to abide by what you believe in. However you will find you lose that right if you ignore your child and do not really listen to his expression of his own feelings. You may have to work extra hard for a while to make sure you are really providing what he enjoys from what is available in your environment. The later you start mixing him with unknown outside contacts, the longer you shelve the problem of his complaints. So it may be worth your while to defer his start at preschool group, otherwise you may find you are against his choices for too much of your lives. On the other hand, it could be argued that the sooner you get used to dealing with what you are eventually going to be up against, the more accustomed you will be to it when the pressure starts really mounting as the child grows older. It's a similar problem to making decisions about TV viewing.

If he doesn't get used to the idea that other people do things differently by the time he is about seven, he may then be enormously resentful that he has been deprived of this information and feel that life has been deliberately kept from him. And anyway, if you are really offering the four- or five-year-old what he needs, there will be no threat (or not a real one) from the consumerist types he encounters. By the time he is a bit older he may even begin to enjoy the differences between himself and others, especially when he begins to understand about the threat to the planet and realises that his life is not only enjoyable but is also geared to doing the world the least possible damage.

The major area, other than toys, food and TV, in which the Green child may differ from his peers is clothes. On the whole, his are probably secondhand. There is no reason why he should not know this – or why he should know. Shopping for clothes is not an activity you need to share with your children, if you know their sizes. The longer you put off taking them, the less you will have to spend and the less arguments you will have. Obviously, if you have some needlework skills, you will be able to make many of their clothes. Provided you have some feeling for what the child likes, if he is not used to excess clothes he will probably be delighted with any 'new' garment you find or make for him. If it is wildly unlike what most of his peers are wearing he might just be teased, so drastic differences should be avoided. But on the whole, clothes for children of this age can quickly be altered if necessary. There are parents who, by the time their children are three or four, are being dragged by their children round dozens of shops until they find 'exactly' what they want – which often doesn't exist. It's all rather time-consuming. In any case, if we do not want our four-year-olds to become involved with fashion consciousness, we should neither start giving them early choices or leaving our glossy magazines around if we happen to read them. They can have their go at fashion later, if they must (it would be barmy to try to influence their tastes during adolescence, unless we want a revolution on our hands).

There is a time and a place for children to start to make their own choices in matters which, like footwear, affect major aspects of life such as health and the family bank balance. But children, unlike animals, are not ready to leave the nest either physically or mentally for several years; nature has provided parents to take care of them and, however democratic we would like to be, we must be willing to guide firmly. This does not always happen, even where shoes are concerned. Several shoe shop assistants I spoke to said that in their experience, most children were perfectly happy with 'a new pair of shoes' but that an increasing number of very tiny children now seemed to be dictating terms, whether or not the parents thought the shoes suitable or could afford them. In the long run this is not fair to the child. However, they must learn to choose, so a limited choice would seem a sensible option.

The period of middle infancy discussed in this chapter is the last part of the child's life when, for most of the time, home is the principal authority. Once the child is at school the need to compromise our ideals with outside pressures is immeasurably greater. The less we compromise when we do not need to, the more we can give way later if we have to, as we are less far down the slippery slope to start with. And it's no fun allowing things to happen which we don't believe in.

## ORGANISING FOR ACTIVITIES

All the creative activities mentioned in this chapter are far easier if some initial organising is done. People have said to me, 'I don't have old loo rolls, bits of cardboard, pipe cleaners, etc., handy. It makes a mess to keep them.' But this elementary recycling and multiple use of objects is very important for the child to grasp.

You do need some kind of system if you are not to be swamped by bits and pieces, though. If you have a large box, drawer or shelf, full of bits and pieces that the children can use, labelled 'making things', you can just chuck in useful bits of material, old boxes, old cards, etc., when you come across them. Playdough can live in bags in the fridge, and will keep for many months. Eventually, if you can find the time, you and the children can sort out the 'making things' stuff, and classify it into smaller boxes. Children like doing this, and it makes life incomparably easier.

Here is a list of useful basic materials, many of which have already been mentioned.

- Sellotape, glue, paste.
- Scissors, stapler, string, paperclips.
- Pencils, paper, paint.
- Huge cardboard boxes – for dens, etc.
- Old curtains, blankets, etc. – also for dens, beds, etc.
- Old plastic bottles – make skittles, people, bracelets, quoits, squirters.
- Bricks.
- Old cards, magazines, etc.
- Old buttons, bits of ribbon, wrapping paper, corks, bits of wood, egg cartons, plastic containers, cotton reels.
- Materials for simple cookery.
- Dice, for games like snakes and ladders – two dice speed up the game, and they learn simple addition without tears.
- Playdough.
- Acorns, conkers, leaves, leaf skeletons, bark, twigs, sticks, stones, feathers, etc. that they find on the ground.
- Books, dolls.
- Washing-up bowls, water, sand.
- Bats, to go with balls – you can easily make some simple ones.
- Several types of elastic – for masks, spinning toys, altering dressing-up clothes.

- Stories to read and tell them.

And a few toys, if they are needed. Very good deals can be had at bazaars, jumble sales, garage and car boot sales, so they can be recycled toys and need not cost much. But don't be tempted to buy a lot just because they are cheap; the point is not to save money but to keep life simple and to enjoy making much out of little.

## FURTHER READING

*Contrary Imaginations*, Liam Hudson, Methuen, London, 1966. Good introduction to the concepts of lateral and convergent thinking and their uses.

*Play: Its Role in Development and Evolution*, edited by Jerome Bruner, Alison Jolly and Kathy Sylva, Penguin, London, 1985. An enormous book, dealing with all aspects of the subject in essay form. Good for both theory and practical ideas, although the practical side is not the main aim of the book.

A good nursery rhyme book – songs and poems are not only fun to sing, but they help speech and, later on, spelling.

A good making things book – see end of Chapter 4.

The Thimble Press, Lockwood, Station Road, South Woodchester, Stroud, Glos GL5 5EQ publish a number of very useful pamphlets about approaches to books and reading with children. Write for a catalogue.

# 7.
# GREEN
# EDUCATION

Private or state, local or remote, formal or informal, what school can I find that will really suit my child? Apart from those parents who live in an area where there is no choice, all parents find themselves asking these questions and never – quite – finding the perfect answer. The choice of school can cause tremendous heartache, and is enormously important. The child is going to have to spend every day there for years, and the education he receives there may prove extremely valuable in the development of his capacities and his career choices later in life. Although it is quite possible to catch up on missed qualifications as an adult, it is much easier not to have to. What will be discussed in this chapter are the problems of schools, the question of how far their philosophies fit in with a Green outlook, and some of the considerations that the Green parent might find useful to take into account either when choosing or when attempting to influence the policies of a school.

It is easy to criticize schools. Underfunded, under-resourced, bombarded from all sides by new policy requirements, new examination demands, the vicarious whims of local and national government, the concerns of parents and employers ... Schools have become battlegrounds where daily the values and practices of an older, established order try to fend off the relentless and unco-ordinated attacks spawned by the disorder and challenges of the late twentieth century ... All of these new challenges, of course, have repercussions throughout the global system and implications for the future of the planet which may well go far beyond our present understanding.

S. Greig, G. Pike and D. Selby, *Earthrights*
from the Centre for Global Education

## WHAT CAN WE REALLY EXPECT FROM SCHOOLS?

It is perhaps remarkable that so many schools do manage to sustain a genuine love of learning in some of their pupils. Some of them also help pupils to think, and raise their level of self-esteem. More of them probably could if they had sufficient funding to be differently organised, and also if their reforms and parents' wants were more in tune with each other. Unfortunately, however, it is extremely difficult for us as parents (however little we enjoyed our own schooling, or however little we really got from it) to be wholeheartedly supportive of radical change. We are products of one form of education, and to admit that our own type of education might not be the best for our children, or for the present-day world, we would have to rethink some of our deeply-held assumptions about education.

We may well be forced to do this in the end if we do not do so willingly, now. Our education took place long before there was a general awareness of the problems now facing the planet. It educated us for a society that has exacerbated those problems, although that was neither the fault of the education nor of us, since these problems were foreseen by very few. Nor was so much then known about the importance of inner motivation and its connection with high self-esteem in the child, the importance of which has been discussed in earlier chapters.

By their nature, children are programmed to learn. They are naturally motivated to do what seems useful or desirable. No child needs to be taught to walk or talk, except in cases of severe handicap. Some conditions are more favourable to their learning than others, and they benefit from the right kind of help and encouragement. Most teachers genuinely want to help them to learn. However, for many reasons, they can never provide the optimal conditions in which the child's learning can take place. Firstly, they are dealing with large numbers, in most cases. If there are 25 children in a class (which is small by present-day standards) and there are 25 teaching hours in a week, the average time available to each child is one hour a week. So finding out enough about each child to provide him with highly motivating tasks is an impossibility, particularly as the child's interests will change. Cooperative learning is, happily, increasingly a part of primary school methods, and much motivation is provided by the interactions within the group. Group organisation enables the teacher to be free from the need to teach the same thing to the class at the same time, although this is still a part of the day's activity in very many classes.

There is a need for a considerable amount of order when dealing with a large number of small children. And while there are some teachers who seem able to restore order to a chaotic class simply with a meaningful smile, there are a great many more who can't, or who think they can't, and whose only alternative is to run the class on much more formal lines. Getting 30 children of completely different abilities and interests to copy the same set of words from the blackboard will certainly result in an ordered classroom. But it will only be an appropriate task for about one-third of the class; the quicker children will be bored, and the slower ones will be lost. And what can this activity mean to a small child? What does school look like? What happens when a child goes into his first infant class?

## THE CHILD IN THE INFANT SCHOOL

On her first day at school the child is probably very excited, and may have been up since some ungodly hour like 5.30, dressed and ready. If she is at a uniformed school she will probably be dressed in a fairly dreary colour, but will naturally be proud of her grown-up smartness. However, the uniform itself is an inhibitor; she cannot feel as free in it as she would in a T-shirt and trousers. She and her mother arrive at the same time as all the other new mums and children; some of the mums stay (and maybe the two dads who are there), and some of them go. Some of the children look pretty unhappy when their mothers go; unfortunately mothers have been told that going to school can be very traumatic for the child and so they cannot help but project their own anxieties on to the children.

The room is decorated with symbols demonstrating the priorities of this subculture. Books predominate, and there are alphabets and sentence builders, lots of symbols of literacy. There are also toys, mostly educational ones, and a 'home corner' like the one at nursery. The teacher gets them all sitting down, at desks or tables in some schools, and on a carpet in others, and takes the register. Some more of the mothers leave. If she has not done so already, the teacher introduces herself (or himself, if the school is lucky enough to have one of the minute number of men who opt for this job). Then she may, to homogenise the class and start the day calmly, tell them a story, one specially chosen to be suitable for children of this age. Next she may divide them into groups and set them a task to do. Although many infant classes allow a good proportion of time for the children to adapt to their new circumstances by playing freely with each other, there are normally tasks prescribed which help them to settle and, by her observation of the child's performance, help the teacher to see how the child might work best.

Towards the end of the morning the class may watch a television programme, like 'Words and Pictures', in which things that the teacher could have done herself are instead performed on a screen. However, the virtues of these series have been extolled for so long that their use is no longer in question; and anyway, switching the television on is a marvellous way of keeping them fairly constructively occupied. Whatever the educational value of the programme, the teacher needs the break.

The children have lunch, supervised by more strangers. With luck it's a tasty lunch, and with more luck it isn't short of nutritive value. Then the children go into a crowded playground full of other small children shrieking and racing around to use up the surplus energy that has had to be contained in the classroom. Some of the children appear very tough, some are just plain frightened, and some are wandering around aimlessly because they have no idea what to do with themselves if they are not actually provided with something to do.

After lunch the children are told another 'suitable' story, then they have to undress down to vest and pants for 'PE'. One or two of the children may not want to do this – most adults probably wouldn't want to strip off in front of a crowd of strangers – but they want to please the teacher. So they do it, hating it and weeping internally, and they suppress their misery because they don't want to be seen crying. In a few weeks they will no longer think of the teacher's request as unreasonable; they will have learned that conformity saves trouble.

One day a week the child may be allowed to bring in a toy from home. She may have been quite happy before with her cardboard-box garage and her well-loved, modest, cloth doll, but they will look pretty silly next to Joshua's remote-control car and Lucy's life-sized, fashionably clad crying baby doll. It doesn't take her long to feel ashamed of her home-made offering and to be asking mother for more toys, many of them symbolic of military aggression (boys' toys) or gushing sentimentality (girls' toys). Even if there is not a toy day at her school, she will shortly be invited to the homes of new toy-imperialist friends (see Chapter 6).

Despite all these obstacles, most infants do learn at school, and sometimes become quite excited about some of the activities. But even, or perhaps I should say especially, when they are excited, they may end up quite frustrated. For it is, often fairly, assumed that the children will be unable to concentrate on a single activity for any appreciable length of time. In making this assumption, and in catering for it by the provision of a huge variety of resources, the child is being encouraged to flit mentally rather than working something right through and making much of little. And whatever her proclivities, there are certain skills which she is expected to develop at a certain time. The child who wants to spend all day drawing so that she can work something out cannot therefore be allowed to do so. Even if the teacher cannot see any reason why she should not, because she knows she will develop her other skills when she is ready to do so, the system prevents it. For the teacher will periodically have to fill in records of all aspects of the child's development, and she knows that many parents would be unhappy if, for example, the only attribute the child had developed in her first term was intense concentration.

Thus a great deal of frustration can be engendered in the infant classroom, as is obvious from the behaviour of the children when they are coming out of school. Because of their paucity of space, and their high pupil–teacher ratio, the school environment tends to ensure that most children are never quite doing what they are really interested in, or knowing why they are doing it (except to please the teacher), or working right through what they need to work through (and neither are most teachers). Much of their responsibility, individuality and exuberance has to be denied them for the sake of order. And unfortunately, the creation of order often involves a subtle, disguised coercion which may be sowing the seeds of compliance and even withdrawal in the child.

The child in the poem in the box, before he started school, had already suffered because he had never been able to find anyone who would really listen to what he was trying to communicate (a problem he shares with many children and adults). But at least, when he starts school, he has an understanding of himself. And his teacher is not totally unsympathetic; she does not make him wear a tie. But he knows, after the drawing episode, that he might as well give up being himself.

This may seem an extreme statement. But it is a feeling many of us have experienced, if not in the context of the school, in other contexts. However hard parents have worked to build up a child's self-esteem, there is always a risk that it may suffer at school. And the suffering may not be caused by an insensitive remark by a teacher. It is equally likely to be caused by the child's perceived failure at the school's major goal – literacy. For however similar the infant classroom may seem to a nursery classroom, it has one major difference. That difference is the importance accorded to books and the written word. One of the infant school's prime functions is to equip the child with the basic tools of literacy. Literacy is the beginning of power, and we want our children literate.

---

He always wanted to say things. But no one understood.
He always wanted to explain things. But no one cared.
So he drew.

Sometimes he would just draw and it wasn't anything.
He wanted to carve it in stone or write it in the sky.
He would lie out on the grass and look up in the sky
and it would be only him and the sky and the things
inside that needed saying.

And it was after that, that he drew the picture.
It was a beautiful picture. He kept it under the
pillow and would let no one see it.
And he would look at it every night and think about it.
And when it was dark, and his eyes were closed, he
could still see it.
And it was all of him. And he loved it.

When he started school he brought it with him.
Not to show anyone, but just to have it with him like a
friend.

It was funny about school.
He sat in a square, brown desk like all the other
square, brown desks and he thought it should be red.

---

And his room was a square, brown room. Like all the
other rooms.
And it was tight and close. And stiff.

He hated to hold the pencil and the chalk, with his arm
stiff and his feet flat on the floor, with the teacher
watching and watching.
And then he had to write numbers. And they weren't
anything.
They were worse than the letters that could be
something if you put them together.
And the numbers were tight and square and he hated the
whole thing.

The teacher came and spoke to him. She told him to
wear a tie like all the other boys. He said he didn't
like them and she said it didn't matter.

After that they drew. And he drew all yellow and it
was the way he felt about morning. And it was
beautiful.

The teacher came and smiled at him 'What's this?' she
said. 'Why don't you draw something like Ken's
drawing? Isn't that beautiful?'
It was all questions.

After that his mother bought him a tie and he always
drew airplanes and rocket ships like everyone else.
And he threw the old picture away.
And when he lay out alone looking at the sky, it was
big and blue and all of everything, but he wasn't
anymore.

He was square inside and brown, and his hands were
stiff, and he was like anyone else. And the thing inside
him that needed saying didn't need saying
anymore.

It had stopped pushing. It was crushed. Stiff. Like
everything else.

in *Earthrights*

## READING

Debates have raged for years about how children should be 'taught' to read. Millions of pounds have been spent by schools on new systems, in the hope that they might be an improvement on previous systems. Publishers have capitalised on this constant search for improved methods with the production of a vast number of so-called reading schemes. The way these are now marketed is very clever; instead of having, say, six stories of graded difficulty in one volume, the volume is essentially part-published in booklets, at much greater cost, which are said to make reading more accessible to the child than book-like books would.

Such schemes are profitable to publishers, because their sequences are designed to make the purchase of an isolated book from a scheme pointless; several must be bought at once. They are useful for the teacher because she will be asked to provide assessments of how well the child can read and she can use the reading schemes as a measure. But much recent research has indicated that they are, in many cases, more of a hindrance than a help, and that the child is more likely to learn to read for meaning if she is interested in the contents of the book and can see some point in reading it.

The world is full of failed readers, and probably always will be until norms are relaxed, children allowed to proceed at their natural pace and reading is introduced at the appropriate time in each child's development. The British teach reading much earlier than most other countries, and yet they have, relatively, a very low functional literacy rate. This would suggest that it might be worth asking the same question that Greens ask about industry and roads and material possessions – might less (reading years) actually be better than more?

If we want our children to value their own firsthand experiences, and to enjoy cooperation, we probably need less emphasis on books. For books, while useful and enjoyable, can only deal in secondhand experiences. Many of us who were brought up to regard books as providing the answers to almost everything took years to believe that our own experiences and observations were as valid as those which we read about. For example, there is an authority to the cookery book's precise definition about how to make a cake, which can blind us to the fact that it doesn't matter if we get the proportions of the ingredients slightly different. Our cake may not come out with the same texture as the cookery book's cake, but it is equally legitimate as a cake and may even taste better.

And books can make it possible to pass examinations without knowing what the subject is really about – just knowing a bit about somebody else's experience of it. Shakespeare wrote plays for people to see, but generations of people have passed examinations on Shakespeare without seeing what they were writing about. Sometimes they may have spent more time reading other people's commentaries than looking at the actual text.

Furthermore, if books are available, people who could and would happily give advice or help are often deprived of the opportunity to do so. This diminishes human contact and demeans the knowledge of the man in the street. Thus books help us to forget our mutual interdependence and the possibilities of benefiting directly, face to face, from each other's experiences.

## THE PLACE OF DIRECT EXPERIENCE

Step inside and smell the sheep nuts. Reach out of the window and touch a blackbird's nest. Dip a net in a pond and find a rare palmate newt about to give birth.

This is Coombes infants' school in Arborfield, Berkshire, where children learn to add up by picking 840 daffodils (seven each) for Mother's Day and where on Monday morning a six-year-old's story began: 'The lambs were born in the night. I touched Tim's lamb on the nose and it licked my finger.'

From reception, children aged five to seven are steeped in the natural cycles of life, from making compost with leaf litter to planting osiers for basket weaving. 'You can't teach about compost from a work card, can you?' says headteacher Sue Humphries, who wants her children to understand that 'all life starts from the soil and ultimately returns there'.

*Times Educational Supplement*, 10 March 1989

In the present system it seems sadly inevitable that much of what is called education consists of the process of teaching the child not to trust the evidence of her own senses, and not to volunteer original thoughts. However hard teachers may try to allow direct experience, which the so-called progressives do, this fact cannot be avoided. Particularly with younger children, many schools are also trying to teach in a way which is more wholistic than compartmentalised, and which, if continued through the system, would give our children the urgently needed ability to see that everything is ultimately globally linked and that we need to retain an awareness of these links even when dealing with constituent parts of the global system.

Unlike Coombes School, most schools don't have the space to grow 840 daffodils, sadly, although this kind of approach to learning is taken in some city schools. Not only does Coombes school, which deliberately sets out to be Green, give the child an understanding of his place in the natural world, but it provides cross-curricular links without trying. Obviously it is necessary to travel down particular paths in a more disconnected way for detailed examination to take place. The garden may be forgotten while the stamen of the daffodil is studied. But unfortunately, it is usual for the daffodil's origin and place in the garden to become progressively less important as children proceed through the system, and by the time they take their external examinations, knowledge is fairly clearly compartmentalised. A teenager writing an environmental essay that contained detailed knowledge of aesthetics, chemistry, botany, history and land ownership laws could not easily submit it for a qualification unless it was part of a course.

## SCHOOLS, INDUSTRY AND CERTIFICATION

Getting a job is made extremely difficult if the applicant does not have the correct qualifications. Pupils are made progressively more aware of this as they get older; the joy of learning has to be sacrificed to the completion of the syllabus. Miraculously, there are teachers who manage to complete the syllabus and still impart the joy of learning to at least some of their pupils. But the odds are against them. Society wants its finished goods (qualified people) and cannot waive this need to the enjoyment of process. Basically, governments want the schools to equip them with a labour force. So the school system ends up functioning rather like an egg-packing factory, producing care-fully graded products – the 'one-GCSEer' the 'remedial', the 'A-level candidate', the 'Oxbridge possibility', and so on. So even if some primary schools manage to educate wholistically, the constraints on secondaries make it almost impossible. Every-thing, or almost everything, must be tailored to lead up to the examinations sat at 16+.

You would be considered mad if you tried to make all your daffodils and narcissi flower on exactly the same day. No matter how hard you tried, many of them would let you down. And yet it is considered sane to try and make all children of approxi-mately the same age aim for the examinations. Some children will find them easy, and, as it were, aim at them from above. Most children struggle towards them from below. In order to avoid this element of struggle, some private schools have made a practice of leaving these examinations until the children are 17+, when they find that the pupils can complete all the study directly related to the examinations in six months instead of two years. The two years are instead spent broadening and deepen-ing their knowledge in non-examination areas. But these are schools in which the development of reflective abilities is rated higher than speedy development. And, although the parents are aware of the schools' policy when they enter these schools, some of them are not happy about the year's delay. Most of us have been so indoctrinated with the idea of 16+ being the 'correct' time to take these examinations that we would require a considerable mental adjustment to the idea of them being taken later.

The Small School, in Hartland, north Devon, is an example of a school which rejects most of the normal ways of preparing children for examinations (see box on page 110). Despite this rejection, they are, according to a recent report, offering a good education. Most of the children at a school such as the Small School will have learnt not only to pass examinations, but how to go about the business of learning. However, once they have jumped over the 16+ hurdle, they and other people wanting to do anything other than totally unskilled work will find that a 'course' is probably a prerequisite. There is an enormous array of certificates available to prove that a person has 'qualified' in some kind of subject. The proliferation of certification makes it far harder for those who are naturally good at something, or who have a great deal of experience of doing it and who don't need a course, to be taken seriously. 'What is your suitability for the job?' is a question that appears less frequently on application forms than 'Details of relevant courses attended, dates, qualification gained'. Once again, direct experience, insight, self-knowledge, self-teaching ability and personal references are pushed into second place by the need for qualifications. And very many of these qualifications, whatever the quality of the course, do little more than testify to the candidate's ability to do what he is told for long enough.

---

The Hartland school is dramatically different from the average secondary school despite the [Exeter University] report.

The school believes that five O-levels, as long as they include English, maths, a language and a science, are sufficient for entry into most further education institutes. Cooking and cleaning are part of the curriculum and every pupil cooks for the whole school every two weeks. Physical education offers classes in the Alexander technique. Last year the pupils helped to build a workshop at the school. They laid foundations, mixed concrete and built a reinforced wall to hold back a neighbour's garden ...

The curriculum is covered by supplementing the regular staff with specialists from the local community ... so some pupils have learnt needlework and cheesemaking.

*Times Educational Supplement*, 10 March 1989

---

Actually, courses are turning up all over the place now. Lots of them are a marvellous way of meeting other people who share the same interests. Often the students on the courses learn more from each other than they do from the resident expert – but our lack of trust in our own abilities and points of view has been so reinforced during our education that we feel we need an 'expert' to help us. Even relationships are the subject of courses; our lack of self-trust leads us to need to be taught to do what must be one of the most fundamental inherent capacities of man – to get on with each other. Such courses as this are undoubtedly now necessary, probably in increasing numbers, just as are courses on relaxation, but it is an extraordinary reflection on our society and how we have been trained to go about problem-solving and learning that this need should exist.

## TECHNOLOGY AND THE SCHOOL

Our abilities to problem-solve and rely on our own mental machinery are likely to be diminished still further by the very early introduction of high technology into schools. The following advertisement is taken from a teacher's journal, exactly as it appeared. 'Nursery teacher wanted for N ... Modern methods and an interest in computers desirable.' Not at infant, but at *nursery* level. But the computer is not designed for children of nursery age, although many firms are producing software for nursery-age children. The computer is, like a book or a pencil, a tool to be used after an idea has been developed and when calculations too complex for the human brain to handle reasonably need to be done. No infant is going to have ideas that need the aid of the computer (except for handicapped children, for whom the computer can be useful as a communication medium).

---

People's over-dependence on machines and high-technology may be at the root of disasters such as the Purley rail crash.

That was the view of an international group of academics who met at the House of Commons last week to discuss safety, risk and human fallibility ... they shared impressions on a disturbing side-effect of modern technology.

They saw dangerous over-dependence on machines and systems and not on the state of mind and the skills of those who run and maintain them as a growing flaw in our safety culture. Dr David Woods said, 'The ability of technology to prevent disasters has led technologists into the frame of mind that when there is a problem their only answer is to throw even more technology at it.'

*Independent*, 6 March 1989

---

If the computer is merely used as a word-processor, as it is in many schools, the message it gives is about presentation. The child likes to see his work looking important. But what he actually needs is to realise that his own idiosyncratic handwriting, which is what distinguishes him from other people with their own idiosyncratic handwriting, is much more important than what a printer can produce. His work, on printout, is a clone of everybody else's and it is this sameness that he is encouraged to be enthusiastic about. He may, while involved in this use of the computer, learn to become dependent on, and to adopt the standards of, a high-tech machine and not of humanity.

In any case, there is mounting evidence that VDU screens can affect the health of adults, so one can only surmise that they might have similar, or worse, effects on children. Furthermore, machine-dependence is now beginning to show its adverse side-effects, so to start becoming machine-dependent in the early years at school could prove disastrous.

Learning to use a computer later rather than sooner has not prevented anybody who could think from becoming highly proficient at it. There is no reason to suppose that early familiarity with computers will improve the skills of the users, any more than early familiarity with books has increased literacy skills. The development of ideas and thought, and of reasons to use the tools of books and machines, would seem an infinitely more appropriate and effective way for very small children to be spending their time.


## EDUCATIONAL PHILOSOPHY

Before looking at the ways Green parents might think about their child's education and schooling, I should like to look at some of the research that has been done in the development of educational ideas which take into account the specific needs of both person and planet. The Centre for Global Education in York is one such research body, and in its book *Earthrights*, which is written by its team, it summarises its aims.

All of these are aims which are fostered in Green homes; all are aims which we could seek to encourage in our schools. But their achievement in schools will require a radical overhaul of the ideology and system of education, and since education, to date, has mainly serviced the prevalent social and economic system, we cannot expect changes to happen quickly. Meanwhile we can comfort ourselves with the thought that the confident Green child from a supportive background will be able to cope with whatever he is faced with.

It is clear that an appropriate education will have an holistic approach to learning; education will be regarded as a life-long process in which schooling plays an important part, home and the community providing educational experiences for young people. Within school itself, attention will be paid to the whole school experience of a student, not just her academic achievement; similarly, aims such as those outlined below will be regarded as applicable right across the curriculum, not only in the humanities or social studies areas.

1. *Systems*
   Students should understand the systemic nature of the world.
   Students should understand the principles of ecology.
   Students should understand the relationship of person to planet.
   Students should recognise the extent of their potential.

2. *Perspectives*
   Students should recognise that their worldview is not universally shared.
   Students should be receptive to other perspectives.
   Students should appreciate what other cultures have to offer.

3. *Conditions*
   Students should understand global conditions, trends and developments.
   Students should have a concern for justice, rights and responsibilities.

4. *Actions*
   Students should recognize the implications of present choices and actions.
   Students should develop the action skills necessary for constructive participation in global society.

   Greig, Pike and Selby, *Earthrights*

## CHOOSING A SCHOOL

Many of us have no real option about where our children go to school, either for geographical or financial reasons. However, even those who cannot or will not afford private schools do often have a limited choice. But however great the choice, most schools cannot, by their nature, begin to do much more than approximate to a few Green ideals.

The first step is to decide which of your ideals you would be happiest to compromise. If you want them at the local school, which means they use little transport, can travel safely on foot or bike, and accords with Green ideals of community, do you really want them sitting in navy-blue uniforms chanting French verbs? Does a local network count above a more progressive education? If your nearest nearly-Green school is a fee-paying one, are you happy to opt out of the state system without feeling guilty about it? The school just up the road has a marvellous atmosphere, but the exam results are less than wonderful. Do you really mind, or are you confident your child will do well enough anyway? If the academic curriculum seems good but there is a shortage of extra-curricular activites, are you happy for the child to make up the deficit out of school, or would you rather choose a school which provided plenty of extra-curricular activity, even if at the expense of academic standards?

It can really pay to shop around fairly seriously. This means looking at schools during their working day, not merely relying on hearsay. It also helps if you talk to children who are at the schools, and to parents whose opinions and values you respect. Just because your child is capable of getting a scholarship to a prestigious private school is no reason for sending him there (if he is academically that good he'll do well wherever he goes, anyway). Life will be much easier for both you and the child if the values of the school you choose are not opposed to your own values, for such opposition of values will be a daily cause of conflict for both of you.

Looking round a school is a difficult business. In any school, there will be many things going on that you don't like. You may not immediately see the virtues of a school. See if you can go twice, once for initial impressions and the second time after you have had time to think about these impressions and the impressions you have received from other schools. Although no decision on choice of school is irreversible, it saves a lot of trouble to get it right first time. The child is likely to be there for five to seven years, so it does matter.

Obviously, within the Green philosophy mentioned at the beginning of the book, discussing the importance of nurture and care must be a feature of the school. The way in which a school is looked after – its physical appearance – is one way to judge. But just because it is shabby does not mean that it is not staffed by caring people. It may have a good pastoral system, and easy communication with parents. If the school cares in the way you would like it to care, it will probably suit your child at least as well as any other school would.

Everybody has the option of educating children out of school, for all or part of their school career. If you feel that five is too early an age to start, you can keep them at home provided you can show the local education authority that they are being satisfactorily educated, which is not very difficult to prove. Obviously, the longer they are kept out of institutions, the less dependent they will be on them. However, they may find it difficult to adjust when they do finally join the system.

Some people take children out of school at some stage during their school career because they want to travel, or because the child is having difficulties, and there is no evidence to suggest that such children fall behind in their development (many find that studying outside an institution actually puts them academically ahead of their contemporaries, which is not surprising, since their programme has probably been tailormade). Ultimately, anybody with a good basic knowledge of their own language, the use of their imagination, some maths, the ability to think and research on their own, and the full use of their senses, is potentially capable of doing almost anything they want to if they apply themselves. But without maths they are denied science, without language the humanities, without thought and research skills they are teacher-dependent, only able to learn from the prepackaging of schools and courses. They do need the basics.

The reason why the schooling of the Green child, while worth careful thought, need not be a major cause of worry is that if she has always been encouraged to look and listen, to think and to believe in what she is doing, she will be confident about learning and resistant to indoctrination. Her ability to examine the assumptions of what she is taught is important, because she is being taught in school for several hours a day, for anything up to

15 years, so her critical and exploratory skills can become ground into submission, along with her imagination, because of the enormous quantity of information she is expected to assimilate. But even if she is at a school that is poor in Green terms, she can be encouraged to make the most of what is worthwhile. And anything else that is missing can be made up for elsewhere.


FURTHER READING

*How Children Learn,* John Holt, Penguin, London, 1970. A classic – very helpful. *How Children Fail,* Pelican, London, 1969, by the same author, is equally good but perhaps more negative.

*Dibs: In Search of Self,* Virginia Axline, Penguin, London, 1964. A moving and instructive care study.

*Earthrights,* S. Greig, G. Pike and D. Selby, Kogan Page, with the World Wide Fund For Nature, London, 1987. Particularly useful for anyone who wants to try to influence school policy; isolates many points for consideration.

*Why Don't Teachers Teach Like They Used To?,* Rachel Pinder, Hilary Shipman, 19 Framfield Road, Highbury, London N5 1UU, 1987. An excellent analysis of teaching traditions and justification of modern methods.

*Anything School Can Do, You Can Do Better,* Maire Mullarney, Fontana, London, 1985. The story of a very large family who learned at home. Useful ideas, even if your children are in school.

*Deschooling Society,* Ivan Illich, Pelican, London, 1973. As usual from Illich, a totally new and pretty extreme perspective. Much food for thought, even if you don't agree.

The Advisory Centre for Education, 18 Victoria Road, London E2 9PB will provide information on most things to do with education.

For those wishing to educate their children at home, Education Otherwise, 25 Common Lane, Hemingford Abbots, Cambs PE18 9AN, 0480 63130 (not after 9 pm) and the World Wide

Education Service, Strode House, 44–50 Osnaburgh Street, London NW1 3NN will provide support, materials and advice.

The Montessori Society UK, 26 Lyndhurst Gardens, London, NW3 5NW will tell you about their system and provide postal courses and materials. And you might like to take a look at the work of Rudolf Steiner, whose methods are much more popular in Germany than they are in Britain, but which has a great deal to contribute to the Green approach even if you don't go along totally with his philosophy. Information from Rudolf Steiner House, 35 Park Road, London NW1 6XT.

On VDUs
*VDUs, Health and Jobs*, from LRD Publications Ltd, 78 Blackfriars Road, London SE1 8HF, 1985. Available from the above address for £1.10.

*Terminal Shock: The Health Hazards of Video Display Terminals*, Bob de Matteo, New Canada Publications, 1985.

# 8.
# FROM FIVE TO SEVEN – INTO THE WORLD

## THE CHILD AT FIVE

The five-year-old is a highly competent individual, both physic-ally and verbally. He will, over the next three years, come to resemble an adult much more, both in his appearance and the way he thinks. His manual dexterity is still greater with larger articles than with smaller ones (holding a pencil does not come easily to him) and his legs are still proportionally short. He is becoming aware of the size of the world, but still lives very much in the here and now. He still regards his parents as the supreme authorities on life, although admired older siblings' views may carry more weight than is obvious, and he can adapt happily to them so that they can play together (as with younger siblings) if they are allowed to resolve their minor differences without too much intervention.

The competent five-year-old is a useful member of the house-hold. He can wash up, lay tables, clean and sort (there's nothing like a five-year-old for sorting out a chaotic sewing box), put the shopping away, clean, and garden, mostly without help. His cooking is more limited, although he can use a toaster, make fruit salad, knead small quantities of dough and cut up food more efficiently than before. He can, possibly, even cut bread and make sandwiches and get his own breakfast – if he can reach what is needed. He can water and spray plants, feed the cat, empty the compost bucket if it's not too big, and sort bottles into different colours for the bottle bank. Outside normal household routines, he will be able to grow his own mustard and cress in old egg-cartons, cut and glue, paint and draw, make playdough and plasticine models, build all kinds of construc-tions (including dens for himself), reorganise his road layout and make new bits for it, perhaps even little cut-out men. He can do all this on his own if he has access to suitable materials and is in the habit of using them. He can make his own Christmas and birthday cards, wrap presents, change a sibling's nappy, go down the road to post a letter (if he is tall enough and if the road is safe enough).

If he has watched you reading, making shopping lists, writing letters, etc., he will be beginning to understand the significance of the written word and may even be reading some words. He will be good at helping you make up stories and dreaming up play ideas. He will show the beginnings of numeracy, if he has helped you count out the tomatoes, or decide how many people will be in for tea. He can play – and enjoys – board games of the non-strategic variety, such as snakes and ladders, and card games such as snap, but he is not yet a strategist and is likely to become extremely frustrated with strategic games (although he might begin to understand simple ones such as Happy Families).

However, his competence can be misleading. He is still too young to be given a regular job as part of the running of the household, although some children are. He can't really be expected to remember when to do it if it is left up to him, and if he has to be constantly reminded he will resent the reminder in the same way as an adult would. His help will be forthcoming in answer to a cheerful question such as 'Who wants to help with the washing-up?' or 'Anybody want to help sand this door?' or 'Who wants to help with painting the living-room?' But he won't know it's Wednesday every week and that it's his turn to empty the wastepaper baskets. Regular jobs are better left until later, when he can remind himself from a plan on the wall, so that doing the job comes from his own initiative and not from an adult's.

It does seem an awful pity that just as the child is beginning to be so helpful, so self-sufficient and such good company, he is supposed to go out of the house for six to seven hours of the day, to an institution which, as we have seen, cannot allow him such responsibilities. But to school he generally goes.

There is a common assumption that going to school is a major trauma for the child, which may cause all kinds of problems. It does not need to be but, whether it is or not, it is certainly a culture shock both to parent and child. The previously delightful helpful child who could be treated on fairly equal terms arrives home at 3.30 noisy, over-excited and fairly disgusting – in other words, like the popular image of a small child. He has had, except at the very rare school, no private time and no personal space all day, having had to be in one room with 25 or more other children or in a noisy playground with a hundred others. The teacher will have done her best to compensate for this with 'quiet' activities, but the child is none the less overstressed when he comes in.

## RELAXING AFTER SCHOOL

A large proportion of infants are, at this time of day, parked in front of the television to unwind after school, sometimes for two hours or so, which does not leave much social time before bedtime – this is certainly the commonest solution I have come across at this time of day. I can't see how it can rate as a Green solution, however, since it is encouraging dependence on a machine as tranquilliser. It is equally possible for an adult to put the child on her (his?) knee, give him something to eat and drink, and have a chat with him, or read to him or tell him a gentle story, perhaps something he knows quite well, full of peaceful, quiet images. This is the human solution to stress, and usually much more effective than the mechanical one, in that it will revive the child's energy rather than doping him. (If you are dubious, imagine yourself in a hyped-up frame of mind, and compare what you think might be the effects of a gentle hug/ handhold from a loved one, accompanied by a cup of tea, or a flop in front of the box.) A bath might be another solution. Sitting, splashing, floating and reflecting are activities which children need as much as adults, and in his bath the child is able to assimilate and mentally organise the many experiences he has had during the day, rather than sitting in front of yet another collection of images. Playing with siblings, family or children from his street whom he knows informally are also good ways of relaxing.

One of the reasons why the child is stressed by school is that the amount of free expression he can give to his emotions is necessarily very limited, rather like an adult in an office job. In his home environment the child, like the adult, is free to be himself. This is also a case for not having too many teas with friends organised days or weeks in advance – when The Day comes he may not feel at all at ease with his companion, who is his friend of last month. It is also a strong argument for choosing a local school with local friends, since not only will he feel more at home emotionally when he is there, but he is more easily able to go and play informally, at no notice, with his friend of the day.

There are several directly environmentally beneficial activities that will help the child to recover. An amble along an urban pavement, picking up litter, seeing how many bags you can collect, is gentle, quite interesting and, judging from the faces of passersby, does get people to think. (Rubber gloves or something to pick the litter up with are necessary as a precaution against possible infection.) Gentle gardening, maybe raking over a patch of soil, weeding, planting out, deadheading, raking up dead leaves, are all restorative. Finding leaf skeletons, or just hunting for sticks and stones, can be done either in the garden or in the park, which may also have a playground where the child can revive his real energy or a pond where he can feed the birds and ducks. (Take a container and lots of tolerance, as the child will collect fairly assiduously.) On walks such as these there is plenty of opportunity either to talk or to be silent, and they can be an excellent time for talking the day through – and getting much needed fresh air.

Cooking, whether it be the child helping with your cooking or vice versa, is relaxing and can produce goodies for tea. Making bread and different shaped rolls is one of the easiest shared cooking activities, which children like. The texture of the dough has, I think, something to do with their enjoyment and, unlike other cooking materials, it can only benefit from being pummelled and shaped in all directions. It can become a hillside with holes in it for little dough rabbits to disappear into, a monster mouth eating tiny dough plankton, or almost anything else, and still end up as a tasty and nutritious loaf, since it is almost impossible to spoil it. Dough is a living material. It is exciting to peep under a cloth to see how it is rising, and to learn that it will only work at its own speed, and that a little patience is necessary. Bread-making, the provision of the staff of life, means something to children who, because of its central place in one form or another in most diets, are aware of its importance. To make bread is to be at the heart of nurturing the family.

Some children will happily sit and look at, or read, books, or might like to colour something in. Although there are people who feel that colouring in is uncreative, at this time of day a child needs re-creation.

## RECREATION AND THE CHILD'S LIFE

Recreation is vital to life, as can be seen through the seasons, containing periods of creation and periods when growth appears to have ceased. Human beings need this too. Their most recreative period is, arguably, when they are asleep, although meditators might claim that meditation has an even more powerful recreative effect.

The consumer culture has been extremely successful in turning recreational activities into marketable commodities. The leisure sector of the stock market is extremely profitable, and the media have given new meanings to the concepts of leisure, recreation and entertainment. In the leisure sector there are basically two commodities being marketed — recreational activities, which include the assumption of activity rather than passivity, and entertainments, which effectively mean the mass media (although they have a separate heading in the share price index).

Recreation, while it may benefit from both, needs neither marketed activity nor pure entertainment. It is fun to buy some sometimes, but five-year-olds are on the whole probably better off without much of either. Indeed, the process of a five-year-old exercising his imagination is itself literally recreative; he will take material from his own experience, and will re-work it into new situations. He may recreate situations he has been in, in order to live through them again and make sense of them — anybody who has listened to a game of school, or mothers and fathers, or Thundercats, will be familiar with this process.

This raises the question of the material he uses for his own recreation. There are those who suggest that it is the processing of the material that is important, and that it therefore does not matter what the original material was. This is the argument put forward by those who suggest that television and many toys are, if not beneficial, at least harmless, since the 'child will make his own meanings from them'. But similarly he will also digest excessive sugar if left to his own devices, which will end up making him fat and lazy — the sugar takes up a part of his diet that could be better filled with more valuable and nutritious foods. Reworking dubious material will take up mental and emotional space that could be better filled with more positive material. It is impossible to prevent the negative and second-rate creeping into his life, but it is important to try and keep the balance of inputs weighted on the side of what seems to the parent to be more desirable. If we want a child to spend time thinking about nature, or about other people, there's not a lot of point in giving him Chock-a-Block, Roland Rat or He-Man and Shira. There is other material to feed his mind and soul on. There might even be something worth watching on TV, but if it really is worthwhile, then it is also worth the child's while to have revived his alertness before he watches in order to enjoy it fully.

## COPING WITH PEER PRESSURES

Although you know, and your child knows, how competent he is, and what a vital member of the household he is, his position is very different at school. There he is a very small person in a very big world. Even though the school is likely to do its best to help him with his self-image, he can see for himself where he stands – head and shoulders below everybody else. He will be told what to do and when to do it and, whether or not he can see the logic behind the orders, is in no position to do anything about them. This is true both in the class and in the playground. He may have been delighted that he was 'big enough' to go to school, then internally quite uncomprehending when he is treated rather as he was at nursery. This is the first of many times in his life when his ballooning size and sense of importance will be pricked and burst; the first time is on entry to the infants school, the second time when he shifts to the next school, and so on through college (where second-years will be snooty about first-years) and then in his first job. He is therefore repeatedly subject to unspoken reminders that he is of no importance, can have no control, that somebody else knows better than he does.

At these critical times of life he is therefore in need of great support from home to reinforce his self-esteem. However, there may be a clash with parents' interests, because even those who do not consider it acceptable for both parents of a preschool child to work, accept that this is quite in order once the children are at school. And it is not always easy to find a job or jobs that will allow one parent to be at the school gates at 3.30, or whenever school finishes.

Parents who are absent at this time can get quite out of touch with their children, both because they do not see much of the school and because they are less likely to meet their children's friends and parents – the local community. Not only do they lose out on these contacts, but they also miss many stories that the child might want to recount about what is happening at school; for small children don't store information for later retrieval and communication in the same way as adults. They also miss out on the shared after-school relaxation. Everything has to be saved for the weekend, when parents are often quite tired after a heavy week's work and will have 'things to catch up with' in the house.

Many parents of small children are anxious that their children should be able to develop as many activities and skills as possible at the earliest possible opportunity. This applies not only to five-year-olds, but also to toddlers. So many parents who can afford it buy their five-year-olds swimming, gym, music, art, self-defence, tennis, ballet, tap and any number of other classes, to make sure they don't miss out. Despite the fact that, for example, the leader of the Philharmonia orchestra did not start the violin until he was 12, they are led to believe that only an early start will produce results. Certainly gym and ballet are best started early, but I am reliably informed that seven is early enough to start even the career of a prima ballerina. Penelope Leach, in an article entitled 'Is your child burnt out at seven?', suggests that these routines give the children far too little time for being themselves. To be dependent on the structures of others is to be unable to stand outside the system, for the structure-dependent person has to accept what is on offer. This does not align with the thinking needed for the independent-minded Green.

> A lot of it stems from parents being bored by their small children's company ... But many children are kept so busy with structured activities that were they forced to take a break from them then they have no idea what to do with their time. Rather like workaholic adults.
> Penelope Leach, *Good Housekeeping*, April 1989

Children's company is likely to be boring to the adult if that is the only company there is. It is also likely to seem boring if the parent is continually tailoring her activities to something that she considers suitable for the child all the time. It is less likely to be boring if there is an outside goal that parents and children are pursuing together so that activities and conversations become neither adult- nor child-specific but are simply different activities and perspectives on a mutual goal – in the Green parent's case, possibly the environmental one.

If the child starting school has to deal with the structures that school imposes and then has no time to create his own structures outside school, he is entitled to say, when nothing is provided for him, 'I'm bored' and to expect somebody to jump to attention – entitled because that is what he has been led to expect. If he cannot entertain himself, it is because he has never been allowed to learn to do so. This can make life hell for parents, who have then to become permanent entertainers, chauffeurs, and providers and whose children's company is more likely to be boring because they are only reflecting the parent's own ideas back at them and not presenting ideas and perspectives of their own.

During his first few years at school, the full impact of the difference between your self-reliant Green child and those catered for more by commerce will gradually hit you.

'Why can't I watch "The A-team"?'

'Why don't I get presents between birthdays and Christmas?'

'Why can't I go to America for my holiday?'

Or the child may come home day after day despondent because the other children play TV-based war games and, because he doesn't know the characters, he finds himself with the rotten part and the other children mocking his ignorance. Or everybody else has shoes with a luminous green strip down the side, and your child's sensible lace-ups, which he can manage himself, are pointed at with cruel fingers. Or your daughter comes home in her warm woollen coat saying, with tears in her eyes, 'I need a new coat', which she doesn't – but she does, because everybody else has got quilted cotton coats and she is miserably trying to survive being the outsider.

And all this suffering and misery is coming home to you. You are being faced with your child's need to adopt values you have rejected, or never held – her real need to watch 'Neighbours', to have guns, to take wasteful plastic cartons of drink to school. And you know she loves you really, but there is, at her age, no chance that there in the middle of the huge playground, with the rest of the class laughing at her (or so she feels), she can understand or even remember you and the home she loves so much. Or she may remember it, want her mummy, nothing else; if a boy, he may adopt machismo attitudes in self-defence, tell lies about what he has (but hasn't actually) seen on TV. The child may be split into tiny pieces by this process.

How simple it would be to rush to the shops, buy a coat, a Barbie doll, guns, the shoes with the luminous streak, comply with the next request and the next, until he watches everything on TV until after his bedtime, and he is tired and aggressive. He is then 'one of them'. But you can't let that happen because it is not what you believe, and your child knows it's not what you believe. And if you do give way you have let him down by capitulating, and any firm base of values he may have had has disintegrated, his feet finding no firm ground on which to tread, his toes feeling only the beginnings of a quicksand.

This is when you probably (unless you are super-self-sufficient and confident, and many of us aren't) need support, the support and time of any other parents who feel as you do. For you are going to have to compromise, and in order to do this as painlessly as possible, but sufficiently to allow your child happiness, you will need help in the exchange of ideas. And you also need to know what is really going on. It may be, for example, that there are only one or two members of the class who really do own 20 Transformers, but that they are influential bullies. The only way to find out is by talking to other parents, and then you can point out to your child that 'Paul hasn't, and Johnnie hasn't, and only Matthew and Ronnie have – and do you want to be like them?'

Where, and how, do you compromise? If your child is very strongly involved with you and your values he may be able to stand outside his peer group; there are children who are happy to be different. If this is the case, there is no real problem, although even if the child is happy on his own, most parents hate to think of their children being social outcasts. And the teacher may cause the parents to worry, telling them that their child is not adapting to the group, because the teacher himself may have problems adapting to the self-reliant child, particularly if the child does not conform to what is expected of children.

Teachers have themselves been taught to look for signs of insecurity, to the extent that if a child is too serious or too self-sufficient they may suspect there is something the matter with him. To take an example; one seven-year-old, a keen reader, was getting impatient with the rather lightweight books she was being given to read by the school. The parents went to see the teacher to enquire as to whether there was a school library, with more choice, that she could use instead. 'It is', the teacher said, 'a good idea to read the class books. Children need all kinds of reading, and easy fiction is fun.' This is an example of social definition of what is enjoyable – and is an extraordinarily presumptuous thing to say. The child found the books were not enjoyable and were therefore no fun. I would rather read Jane Austen for fun than Jeffrey Archer, and would be very angry if told that I should have the 'fun' of easy fiction. This non-serious, not very constructive fun-loving mentality is fostered not only by the mass media but also in this way (probably unintentionally) by school.

So if your Green child appears serious at school because he takes school seriously, you may have problems with the school. The current view that fun cannot be had from serious activity is merely a symptom of society's adulation of the trite and superficial. That somebody might actually prefer Dostoevsky to the latest trendy film, partly because of the rewards of the effort of reading it, is hard for anybody to believe in a society which emphasises the virtues of instant rewards and labour-saving devices above all else.

The worries of teachers and parents that the child is not socially adapted can be a strain, even if the parents believe that most of society's values are upside-down, and these worries can lead to great internal conflict. On the one hand the Green parent wants a child who will resist the prevailing set of values; on the other hand, the parent wants to feel that the child is not a social outcast. As so often, the conflict is a reflection of the problems faced by many adults, whether dark Greens, Christians, or any other minority group challenging the dominant culture. Many of us would like our children to be better at being 'different' than we are; we'd like them to be less image-conscious, less susceptible to advertising pressure, less worried about opposing the majority. But we hate to see them alone, and find it hard to believe they might feel more integrated as people than they would if they joined in with the others.

This area is particularly difficult for those who really can afford to buy their children the latest trendy items. But if you give way, your child may become insecure and obnoxious. If you don't give way to him at all, you make his life very difficult, because he is in the invidious position of living with varied sets of values all coming from nice people. Mum, who he believed to be right, doesn't think the same as Matthew's very nice Mum. Who is right? True, the psychological literature suggests that children learn quite quickly that different people do things differently, and that they can easily adapt to what is expected; so they seem to cope fine, without apparent conflict. What is not clear, however, is the long-term effects on the integrity of the personality and the child's eventual resilience.

But you don't have to buy guns on demand. For each age group there are several material possessions and activities, the ownership and doing of which allow the child to be accepted. They are symbols of the child's acceptance of cultural norms. For example, at various times in the late 1980s Transformers, Ghostbusters and accessories, certain kinds of guns, certain computer games, bikes, skateboards (whether or not they could use them), Lego (mostly Space Lego) and watching 'Thunder-cats' and 'Neighbours' were some of the symbols for young children. The Green child does not have to be able to demonstrate his possession of all these goods to be accepted by the others; just one or two act as a passport, which gives the Green parent some leeway. We got away with a (hand-me-down) bicycle and the 'right' shoes for our son, and for our daughter at that age a My Little Pony which served its symbolic purpose but which was hardly ever used. The bicycle we liked anyway, and we chose the My Little Pony because the then alternatives, Barbie or Sindy dolls and Care Bears, seemed to us to convey quite unacceptable messages. Some people don't like their children watching much TV, so they would have to find another symbol. But if you reject all of them (and most of them are affordable if bought secondhand and cleaned up) you are rejecting your child's playground culture, which is a part of him.

Rejecting his friends would probably also be unwise. If he wants to have Matthew to tea and you know of Matthew as a violent little thug, you still owe it to your child to have Matthew, provided he toes the house line (but keep your ear open while they are playing). Although you cannot decide on the nature of the games they play, you can rule out of order any behaviour or items Matthew brings to which you object. If Matthew arrives with his new repeating revolver, you are entitled to acknowledge its arrival and then say 'I'm glad you like it, but I'd rather you didn't use it while you are here – I'll look after it for you.' Or if he arrives, as is becoming increasingly customary, with a video cassette, you can make the same kind of statement; provided, of course, that there is enough else for them to do and that you really are welcoming of your child's friend (which means, for example, providing something really tasty for tea).

If you are too dogmatic in your approach, you may find your child organises himself invitations to friends' houses more and more, so that he can taste the forbidden fruit and become familiar with the common cultural symbols which are denied at home. Non-TV owners sometimes have this problem, and there are some who have bought televisions because they would prefer to know what their child was watching, and watch it with him, than not know. However, if TV does not fit into your family's lifestyle and you don't want to spend the not inconsiderable amount that it costs, you may either have to put up with your child's absence or make what is on offer sufficiently appealing for his friends to prefer to come and do it instead. Either way, there is no reason to feel guilty, or feel that you are depriving your child of an essential part of life. You might, however, have a word with your child's teacher and point out that it may be difficult for your child to talk about his 'favourite programme' if this is used as class material, which it increasingly is.

## CULTIVATING GREEN CONTACTS

The more the child identifies with a group who share your values, the easier life will be for both of you. He is still too young to be able to detach himself from situations and view them objectively, which he will soon be able to do in a way which will help him to understand your point of view and why it does not match everybody else's. Keeping him in touch with like-minded people and really working hard to make sure he is happy during these few years is worth the effort. If you have a group such as Woodcraft Folk near you which he can join, it will help, or a good active after-school club; and if he has a friend from preschool days who is at another school, it may be complicated to get them together but provides him with a sense of security and a like-minded peer with whom he can identify and feel safe.

If you have only recently decided to adopt a Green approach, or want to become darker Green, this may not be easy. If he is accustomed to loud, aggressive, mechanical toys and you suddenly decide to go for low-tech, life-affirming wooden toys, he may take quite a time to adjust since they may seem very feeble, and will demand more of his imagination than he is used to giving. You'll probably have to spend a lot of time playing with him and them so that he develops his ideas about how to use them and enjoy them. Similarly, if you decide that he is watching too much of the wrong kind of television, there's no point in trying to reduce his viewing without having something to put in its place – so you will have to work out why he is watching what he is watching and what would therefore substitute for it. For example, if you don't want him to watch 'Neighbours', he might be happy if he was allowed to see real adults communicating over cups of tea, or he might enjoy some street activity. If he's watching when he gets home from school because he can't think of what else to do, some of the ideas in the section on relaxing after school from the earlier part of this chapter might be helpful. A continuous project, such as building a model farm or forest, which has a little bit added every day, or a cut-out village kit or something similar would substitute for television if it is predictability he needs it for. The garden could be used for similar ongoing, predictable daily activities, and he may then discover the rewards of step-by-step activities.

Throughout her childhood, the child is being introduced to activities which by virtue of their relationship to the spiritual (cooking, playing by herself or with others, nature, gardening, painting, imaginative creation, music, plays, physical exercise, etc.) and their lack of dependence on either high technology or material consumption, make them fulfilling, non-destructive, Green activities which will enhance the individual's and the planet's life. During the next few years she will want to try to learn some of these activities in a more formal setting, and to acquire the disciplines which will lead to more creative and re-creative freedom. The more she sees her parents enjoying them, the more inclined she will be to try. So although I have not mentioned the lives of parents since Chapter 2, I am assuming that they will be continuing with their own life-enhancing activities as much as possible, both for their own sakes and so that their children are provided with models, goals and inspir-ation.

## FURTHER READING

Many activities can be developed from the books and ideas already mentioned.

*Simple Crafts*, edited by Dorothy Ward, Ward Lock, London, 1988. This is a good book to start with if you want more refined craft work. It has lots of ideas and techniques for basic carpentry, raffia work, weaving, leatherwork, for example, and a section on making presents at the end. The materials used are not all eco-friendly, but most are – if not, you may want to substitute alternatives.

*The Reader's Digest Repair Manual*, Hodder & Stoughton Ltd, London, 1972, is also worth familiarising yourself – and your children – with. There's often a fair bit of mending toys, etc., needed, and they can learn too. Try to use less toxic materials where possible; the more magical and instant glues, for example, are the most toxic. Find out what's in them.

*Let's Cooperate*, Mildred Masheder, Peace Education Project; this is not available commercially, but can be obtained by writing to Portland Lodge, 75 Belsize Lane, Hampstead, London NW3 5AU. Contains lots of activities and ideas which will develop self-respect, the ability to play cooperative games, and things to make.

*Sharing Nature With Children*, Joseph Bhanat Cornell, Exley, London, 1979. A beautiful book, full of ideas which a family or group could try out.

*Growing Up To Love Nature*, Elizabeth Stutz, Play for Life, 31B Ipswich Road, Norwich NR2 2LN. A useful pamphlet. This organisation publishes many such pamphlets, mostly at less than £1, including a useful toy catalogue *A Guide to Playthings for Life*. It is a non-commercial non-profitmaking organisation which is well worth writing to; its emphasis is entirely non-violent, and many of the toys it recommends are beautifully made and inexpensive.

Try and get hold of some songbooks; A & C Black have a useful series of books of simple tuneful songs.

# 9.
# FESTIVALS AND SEASONS

> Travelling through the year's festivals with children is like experiencing the rainbow – no sooner has one colour faded than the next one appears. Ceremonies which have their roots deep in mankind's past flower in the day-to-day life of caring which is the home, and can be a source of healing in many troubled times.
>
> Caz Iveson, in *Lifeways*

Festivals are almost the last relic of sacramentalism in the 20th century. This does not mean that they necessarily have religious connotations any more, but that they are occasions marked out by a specific ritual. They can play an important part in our efforts to help ourselves and our children understand our place in the rhythms of the universe. We know the value of ritual and rhythm to small children, which can be seen in the precise ordering of events – the child's bedtime, or the timing of the daily snooze. As adults, the summer holiday is often an annual ritual, as might be meeting Fred every Friday in the pub, or exchanging birthday cards with an old friend we may never see again. Such rituals lend security, continuity and a sense of ongoing meaning to life.

The old traditional festivals performed a similar function, and many of them were associated as much with the passing of the seasons as they were with a religious calendar. These associations can help to remind us of the cycles of the natural world which, if we live in a built-up area, may often seem rather remote.

## EASTER

The annual cycle could begin anywhere. I am going to start at Eastertime, because it symbolises new growth. Like all the other major festivals, this has been commercialised almost beyond recognition. Most of us will find ourselves going through the rituals of chocolate eggs, bunnies, cards, etc., whether we like it or not, so we might as well make positive use of what can hardly be avoided.

The Easter symbol is the egg. (Will it be looked at differently now that eggs are considered such dietary villains?) The hen's egg is one of nature's glories, a rather fragile, classically-shaped case holding the promise of new life. In terms of the promise it holds for children, the egg is a wonderful medium for creativity. A blown eggshell (prick a hole in each end and just blow until the inside comes out – eat it later) is a good medium for paint-work, and its curves seem to enhance almost anything that is imposed on it. It needs care in the painting, but not an enormous amount; small children can decorate eggs beautifully if given the right media (paint, ink, felt-tips, little things to stick on them). Decorated eggs hung up by a thread make fresh, light Easter decorations, and an Easter egg tree can be made by hanging the eggs from twigs. (Tie a knot in some thread and put a long needle right through the holes at both ends.) If a few twigs with leaf buds can be cut and put in water to hang the eggs from, these reminders of spring will gradually open.

Celebratory food can be cooked with the children; hot cross buns and simnel cakes with their marzipan decorations. Cooking for a festival, especially if the food has then to be stored for a while, is a contribution which also adds a certain anticipatory excitement.

There will be some early flowers out, and some shoots coming up in parks, country and garden, and perhaps some early weeds. After Easter (depending on when it falls) is the time to start gardening in earnest, although by now some seeds can have been sown in trays indoors, ready for planting out later. Children who like recording information may enjoy making notes on the progress of their seeds and plants. If you are lucky enough to have a bird nesting-box in a tree, now is the time to look and see what is in it – but not too often, or the mother bird will leave the nest.

## SPRING AND SUMMER

Spring continues with the May Day and Whitsun festivals, which are good times to go for early picnics under the blossom. Late May is a wonderful time for walks in woods; the foliage has not completely developed and is still a bright fresh green, thin enough for the birds to be seen through with a pair of binoculars. As soon as all the frosts have stopped there is more planting out to do, in gardens and windowboxes, or in tubs on balconies, and the hedgerows will be full of wild flowers.

June brings the summer solstice, Midsummer's Day. This is a time for soft fruits and lazy days, unless it's a really wet June, and for making jam from strawberries and gooseberries. Midsummer Day (or the nearest weekend day) is an ideal time for a celebratory outdoor evening meal, with coats if it's chilly, and a late night for the children.

The next great 'festival' for the family is often the summer holiday. For many children this holiday is the only opportunity to spend time away from the urban environment. But commerce and prepackaged holiday entertainments are reducing the child's opportunity just to be himself in a different environment. A typical advertisement 'This summer, let your kids express themselves' is followed by the opportunities Austria offers – 'adventure camps, game parks, kindergartens, alpine zoos', purpose-built structures to replace the chance of just being in the mountains. If children don't meet real countryside or unspoilt seasides now, they may never discover the joys of wilderness and quiet, or the calm of watching waves breaking on a peaceful shore while they aimlessly throw the odd stone in.

The holiday festival finishes when the family returns home, and the children perhaps go back to school. The garden is still full of late summer flowers, and now is the time to pick any vegetables if you have found space to grow them.

## AUTUMN

Around Michaelmas, which is 29 September (around the autumn equinox), chestnuts and conkers begin to fall, and the nights become chilly. A Michaelmas meal, with Michaelmas daisies and some of the vegetables which are so abundant at this season, is a ceremonial beginning to the autumn. It can be preceded by blackberry-picking expeditions – filling pots and bags, getting messily dyed blue, accidentally staining T-shirts, gives a good purpose to an afternoon with a picnic. When you have eaten the blackberry pie the next day, you can start to think about planting bulbs for winter flowering indoors or spring flowering in the garden.

Then comes Harvest Festival time. This is celebrated in most schools, and you can celebrate at home by baking harvest loaves, preparing another celebratory meal and perhaps doing a play. Leaves will have turned on some of the trees and, although they will not keep their colour long in water, can be used to make decoration for the Harvest table (and perhaps then pressed, when they will keep their colours).

## CHRISTMAS

Gradually the leaves fall, the evenings shorten and we arrive at Advent. Once again, the shops will have got there weeks or months before you do. Whether or not you are a Christian, you can hardly escape Christmas. This indoor festival can bring great life to a rather dreary month, and its pre-Christian origin partly had this purpose. Advent for the Christian is a time of preparation. For the non-believer it is a useful time for preparations for a home-made Christmas. Sometimes after Harvest Festival, cakes and puddings will already have been made, with everybody taking a turn at stirring, but there is plenty more to do in December.

Although Christmas is horribly commercialised and it is tempting to reject the festival, it would be a pity not to use the excuse for celebrating and for recontacting old acquaintances with cards. Advent is the time to find the flowers pressed in the summer, to make cards, or to get out last year's cards, paste labels over the signatures, to get them ready for re-use. Those who like artwork can make their own personal cards, and children can try media like potato blocks and woodcuts. Children love making cards, particularly if you can run to a few stick-on stars or a little bit of glitter (no sprays). Wrapping paper can be made; it is quite easy to find someone who will supply you with a stack of old computer paper, and once again potato printers, cut in simple shapes like Christmas trees or hearts or stars, can be used to print up lots of your very own brand of wrapping paper.

But what goes in the wrapping paper? How do we get away

from some of the tat? Advent not only allows time for preparation, but also allows time for Christmas fairs and bazaars run in aid of charity, at which it is usually possible for you and your children to find good presents without breaking the bank. Presented in decorated boxes, quite small items acquire some magic. Home-made fudge, coconut ice, marzipan fruits, marzipan stuffed dates, or small biscuits are gifts which children will enjoy making and which the recipients will enjoy eating. Pomanders (oranges stuck with cloves) are lovely scented gifts to hang in wardrobes. Small cloth bags of home-made pot-pourri (dried scented flower petals) are useful for underwear drawers. Growing flowers which can be dried and given as bunches doubles the rewards of the gardening involved. Or you and the children can have prepared bulbs in pots which will be ready to flower now.

These are all inexpensive, eco-friendly gifts which children enjoy creating. What they receive, or expect to receive, is another question. If you have decided that Christmas and birthdays are their only present times, the presents need to be rather carefully thought out so that the children end up with, for example, enough writing paper and crayons to last. If you are giving games or puzzles, they should be bought with the next year's use in view. But there are bigger dilemmas. If Johnny is getting a computer or his own TV for Christmas, or five videotapes, will your child feel very disappointed with his less luxurious gifts? Once again compromises will need to be made. However, if the festival and holiday period is well prepared for and is warm and memorable, the problem will be less serious. If the children take part in carol singing and street collections; if they have plenty of attention; if they are really involved in preparation and decoration; if they help to make up beds for visitors; if they can have a trip to a local pantomime and a late night to go with it, they will mind less about the missing videotapes and computer games. (Or they will happily settle for one instead of five.)

## WINTER

After Christmas, winter sets in seriously. No more fruit to pick, or conkers to pick up. With luck there might be some snow and ice; cold walks in the mud, with hot crumpets for tea; taking breadcrumbs to feed the birds and ducks, who now really welcome the food, and coming back in the early evening gloom; perhaps getting out some of the shells or feathers collected on the summer holiday, and making things with them – there are many good ways to spend cold evenings.

Some people celebrate New Year's Day, and some Twelfth Night. New Year's Day is a good time to try to change something. A family resolution, like 'We will try not to use plastic carrier bags this year' can be worked out. (Many people, myself included, only manage to stick to their resolution for about a month, but it's better than nothing.)

In January, marmalade oranges appear in the shops. Marmalade making is another annual ritual in many homes, and can involve all members of the family. The smell of oranges cooking fills the whole house for hours while jars are scrubbed and labels made. At the end of the process, there is considerable satisfaction for children to see the jars of marmalade standing in neat rows waiting to be stored. Every time they eat marmalade during the coming year, it will have some meaning for them.

Pancake Day comes next, and provides another excuse both for celebratory eating and for the making of resolutions. Traditionally something was given up at this time, for a limited period, but there is no reason why something could not be taken up instead. (We aren't very good at Lent resolutions either, but there are plenty of people who make their resolution last for at least 40 days.)

Then Lent finishes, and we are back at Easter. The year's cycle is complete.

I have left birthdays out of this calendar, for the obvious reason that they could come anywhere, and not because they are unimportant. The chance to celebrate is a chance to focus on one member of the family, and a chance for everybody else to think about what they can do for the birthday person. Getting into huddles and working out what they might like, what you will cook, what kind of party they want, is rather exciting. Birthdays deserve a place in the family as special as other festivals. Celebrations in general are worth doing wholeheartedly – there is enough around to be miserable about.

FURTHER READING

*Lifeways*, Gudrun Davy and Bons Voors, Hawthorn Press, Stroud, 1983. Many ideas on living as a family. The Hawthorn

Press also publish other books of this kind, as well as craft books, etc. Write for a catalogue to 1 Berkeley Villas, Lower Street, Stroud, Glos GL15 2HU.

*All The Year Round*, Toni Arthur, Puffin, London, 1981. A compendium of games, customs and stories, taking you right through the year and looking at festivals long forgotten. I don't believe anybody who reads this book could ever be bored or would ever really need much else to get them going.

*Advent For Children*, Freya Jaffke, Floris Books, Edinburgh, 1983. Lovely things for children to make when they have got beyond the stage of basic decorations, at about the age of nine or ten, and want to try something more ambitious. Uses many natural materials like sticks, twigs, unspun sheep's wool which you pick up on summer walks and then try and think of a use for. Floris publish many books in the Steiner tradition, and it is worth getting their catalogue – write to 21 Napier Road, Edinburgh.

*Festivals, Family and Food*, Diana Carey and Judy Large, available from Rudolf Steiner Mail Order, 38 Museum Street, London WC1A 1LP, 01-242 4249. Lots of illustrations, recipes, songs, crafts, etc.

*Books of Songs*, Walther Braithwaite, with a foreword by Yehudi Menuhin, has songs for different seasons of the year, for use with children. Also available from Rudolf Steiner Mail Order.

# 10.
# FROM SEVEN TO ELEVEN – CHANGE OF TEETH TO ADOLESCENCE

## CHANGES IN PERSPECTIVES

Round about the age of seven the child visibly stops being a dependent infant. His milk teeth are replaced by his second set, his body assumes the proportions of a miniature adult, and his balance, coordination and dexterity approach the adult level. His thinking appears to change, too, as he becomes more able to detach himself mentally from his immediate situation and to reason in the abstract. He is also beginning to see that there are many different answers to any one question, and is therefore able to start to think independently. His wide social circle and his reading, if he is a reader, will present him with many ideas and standpoints from which he will take what he needs. Although he is still deeply attached to his parents and dependent on them for approval, he is prepared to question what they say and to find approval elsewhere. Even if an admired teacher misinforms him in some way, his parents will still have a difficult job to convince him that she may be wrong and his parents right. If he is confident, he may start to question his parents' and teachers' inconsistencies openly; if less confident, he may become worried by them. As a critic, he can be a very salutary conscience for the Green parent – maybe questioning the use of disposable nappies for the baby, or the need to have such a large car, or the wholesomeness of the food he is eating – and although it may be very irritating to have to justify such inconsistencies, his comments will often be well founded.

He has begun to develop a sense of time and distance, so that he can begin to understand how his actions today can affect long-term outcomes. Unfortunately this awareness may lead him to feel guilty. But rational reassurance from parents can help him to realise that although turning the heat up when he is ill does contribute to the greenhouse effect, it can be justified. However, rather than feeling guilty, he may take a high moral tone and make his parents feel guilty about every packet of slug pellets they buy, even though they are trying to save their organically grown lettuce seedlings.

His emotional involvement and deep concern about what is going on in the wider world, coupled with a suspicion that adults may have got things wrong but that he is powerless to do anything about it, may make him anxious. And it would hardly be a healthy sign if his childhood were clouded by too many such feelings, when he is barely old enough to have a clear view of all the positive offerings of the world. Without a strong positive purpose he is unlikely to have sufficient resources to do more than evade the world's negative aspects, rather than try to remedy them. As an example of this rather negative outlook, on a recent discussion programme about children and television a child of nine was asked why he thought watching 'Eastenders' was better than doing something else. His reply was that it meant he knew all about AIDS and divorce and drugs and all that sort of thing and so 'Eastenders' was a good preparation for life. Unfortunately he did not seem to have any positive interests, which prompted one impatient father to point out that he would be better employed finding out what he did want to do than what he wanted to avoid. Did he know, the father asked, what was worth living for? Or was life just spent collecting mental 'Do Nots'?

From the point of view of the child's purpose in life, and because of his possible anxieties, there is a strong case for limiting his access to the mass media in the home, or for making sure a parent is there to discuss it. There are things that each of us, even an eight-year-old, can do about local and global environmental problems. And, frightening as it may be to think of what goes into our food or our drinking water, we are not all about to die – probably. But the child needs the chance to discuss both the facts and his feelings. He may or may not need reassurance; he may also actually welcome the chance of taking some action. Many adults who would like to act do not do so because they have been taught throughout life that there is nothing they personally can do that would make any difference. And yet people do achieve changes through action. The positive nurturing of the 'I can' mentality is needed to combat the apathy bred by a feeling of helplessness.

This positive attitude can be reinforced if the child becomes a member of an organisation which promotes life skills, competence, love of nature and other Green characteristics. Woodcraft Folk, Brownies, Watch, Cubs, sports and other such clubs and organisations not only promote these skills but provide an oasis where the child will not be assailed by the forces of consumerism or apathy. Also, when street and local playing out seems dangerous, these rather more structured groups provide a safe place where he can mix with his peers, away from his parents, but without the institutional and educational pressures of the school.

## MODERN CHILDHOOD

Many children, such as the 'Eastenders' viewer quoted earlier, have by this age lost their innocence and sense of the world's beauty and are behaving like young adults without having adult knowledge, understanding or sense of responsibility. This unsuitable preparation (suitable preparation for life would be to learn to cope with what affected them directly, now) is a reflection of much of adult life. School is attended to render the pupil employable. College is attended to get the next qualification, not for its joys. The first job, at the bottom of a career ladder, and subsequent jobs on the same ladder, are often preparations for a job nearer the top which the person thinks he might like to do, and for which he is continually striving – but which he may never reach. Finally he retires; but as he has forgotten about living in the present moment, coping with where he actually is, and has probably forgotten what he likes doing, courses are provided during his later working years called 'preparation for retirement'.

Children, however, have been provided with a childhood, a manufactured way of life designed by adults, which deprives them of the responsibilities which would give them a sense of self-esteem and a chance to find out what they want. They don't like it, so they end up with a self-manufactured pseudo-adulthood entirely derived from the media, since they have been

> Something has happened to the image of childhood. A full-
> page advertisement in a theatrical newspaper showing a
> sultry female wearing dark lipstick, excessive eye-shadow,
> a mink coat, and possibly nothing else bears the legend:
> 'Would you believe I'm only ten?' We believe it. For
> beyond the extravagances of show business lies the evi-
> dence of a population of normal, regular children, once
> clearly distinguishable as little boys and little girls, who
> now look and act like little grown-ups. ... At the heart of
> the matter lies a profound alteration in society's attitude
> towards children. Once parents struggled to preserve
> children's innocence, to keep childhood a carefree golden
> age, and to shelter children from life's vicissitudes. The
> new era operates on the belief that children must be
> exposed early to adult experience in order to survive in an
> increasingly complex and uncontrollable world. The Age of
> Protection has ended. An Age of Preparation has set in.
>
> Marie Winn, *Children without Childhood*

excluded from genuine adult life and have no other models.
Children get up in end-of-term entertainments and ape pop
stars whom they have seen on TV, wiggling their pre-pubescent
hips and screaming out lyrics about 'lerv' and 'I got my guy'
which are simply not a part of their genuine inner experience.
They are neither being themselves, nor are they copying real
adults. They have no authentic identity. Many of them may end
up later in life in a psychotherapist's office, trying to discover
who they are, because they have never known what it felt like to
be themselves.

But they could actually benefit both from being allowed their
own identity as children and from being allowed to see how
adults deal with each other. The television moguls were
surprised when the soap opera 'Neighbours', which was
designed for adults, became a clear number one hit with
children. Its popularity is surely an implicit statement by
children that what is considered suitable for them is not what
they actually prefer to watch. It would suggest that they really
want to know about the concerns of older children and adults, of
which, in our age-stratified world, they have very little experi-

ence. The antidote to this alienated condition is to let them into our ordinary but fascinating world, not to sit them in front of the remote and over-dramatised world of painted women and fast-talking, aggressive men.

Many parents either wish their children would not watch programmes such as 'Dallas' or ban them from doing so. The lifestyle it presents is probably not one which a Green parent would wish for himself or his children. However, to stop your child watching what 80 per cent of his class is watching is not an easy task. As when dealing with smaller children, informal support networks and even agreements can be invaluable to parents. However, as the child gets older, parents become increasingly less likely to meet each other if they have not done so already. One answer would be to become involved in local groups or the activities of the school in order to find support. And if you, as a parent, are worried about speaking out or seeming different, it is worth remembering that there is usually at least one other parent who feels the same as you, but who doesn't want to be the first to speak out. Often, once one person has spoken up, others are extremely relieved to be able to share their feelings. One way to do this would be to instigate a relevant discussion at a school parents' association meeting, and to develop friendships later with those who are obviously like-minded.

## HELPING THE CHILD TO FORM JUDGMENTS

The child's wider awareness of the world, and knowledge that other people may be as right as his parents, makes him both more susceptible to outside pressures and rational enough to understand his parents' point of view. At seven, he can understand the problems being caused by the destruction of rain-forests, and he can also understand that much of this destruction is caused by the need for land to farm meat for hamburgers. So if you don't take him to McDonalds when he asks, he will understand why not, even if he would still like to go. During these years he will gradually come to understand many of the reasons for his family's behaviour patterns, which he has previously had to accept as he found them. He may decide that many of the reasons are poor ones. Parents could rule his arguments out of order, which might save trouble in the short run but which demonstrates no respect for his desire to understand and to express his own view. Or they can reconsider their own views in the light of how they appear to be affecting him. Many parents may find themselves having to renegotiate their own decisions with themselves. How serious is it if he wants to read comics? What will the effects really be? Does this issue matter all that much, or has it been a point of principle? If so, does it need re-thinking?

You may also have to negotiate with the child. 'If I buy you one gun, are you prepared to do without more?' You have to assess for yourself how much he would really miss having one. Is there something else less warlike that might serve as an adequate replacement? If the child always has a small sum of cash for birthday and Christmas presents to which he can add his pocket-money later, he has the option of buying for himself things that you don't want to buy him. He then has to assess his own needs, and is allowed to be responsible for at least some of his purchases. Also, if you have a 'no presents except at birthdays and Christmas' rule, he can meet his own needs in between. And he is able to assert his own tastes, which he knows are not yours.

However, even if he does buy an article which you do not care for, he must be allowed to enjoy it without having a constant sense of parental disapproval. (This isn't always easy, unless you are very good at being an observer rather than a judge.) Possessions of all kinds should be looked after, treasured and loved. Furthermore, he must be able to respect his own judgment, and make his own mistakes if he needs to.

You can help him to develop his judgment of media-given information without lecturing or being doctrinaire if you sit down with the child and look seriously at a few news stories and advertisements in newspapers and on television. The junior school child is quite capable of understanding that a great deal of what is given out as information is often heavily biased, and, in the case of advertisements, nothing more than an attempt to sell what is unnecessary. If the child looks at lots of the increasingly common advertisements for cleaning agents, and looks at the few cleaners you use, he will see that the huge variety is unnecessary. You may have to explain why most of them are environmentally harmful. To demonstrate the profiteering of branded products, you can show the child the labels on, for example, different branded versions of paracetamol, then show him the generic version and compare the price and the packaging. He doesn't need to be told the conclusions; he will see them. Once he understands this selling process, he is in a position both to defend himself against it and to avoid being imprisoned by its demands. He may even become scornful of it – he will not be the fool who gets tricked by people trying to make him waste his money.

## GREEN ACTIVITIES

If the family has only just decided to start to try to live a Greener way of life, the children can be involved in the discussions and decisions that you may be making. It would be unreasonable to expect anybody suddenly to start enjoying wild-forest walks when they are accustomed to theme parks, or to stop taking individual cartons of fruit juice to school daily when they always have done so, or to tolerate patched or remade clothes when they have got used to spending hours shopping for the latest fashions. But as they begin to understand the reasons, see their parents becoming happier, and discover that their parents now have more time for them, they are likely to want to change too. If there is no Green activity group available, you could start some kind of regular group activity for them and their friends. This would take some thought and preparation, but most children of this age are happy to start on any new activity to which they have not previously had access. Among the activities you might try are:

- Gardening, indoor and outdoor.
- Cooking real meals.
- Camping for a weekend.
- Whole-day walks with a picnic.
- Nature trail walks.
- Museum trips.
- Sewing and knitting – making shopping bags, making clothes.
- Running a sale for charity.
- Playing cards or similar games (there are lots of environmental ones).
- Playing music, or singing.
- Putting on a play for parents and friends, or for charity.
- Experiments in mending, learning repair skills.
- Making things – Christmas cards and wrapping paper, building models.

FROM SEVEN TO ELEVEN

- Doing something for somebody else, e.g. helping an old lady with her shopping.
- Playing with a handicapped child once a week.
- Litterpicking, and campaigning about it in school.
- Bird watching and feeding, bird tables and drawing.
- Wildflower spotting and drawing.
- Writing letters to relevant people about local environmental problems.

All these activities could be described as eco-friendly and a group could easily be run as follows, on a four-week rota:

Week 1  Cooking and gardening.
Week 2  Nature walk.
Week 3  Sewing and games.
Week 4  Music and drama (invented by the children).

Or you could spend two or three weeks doing the same thing – the children will know what they'd like, and will end up doing it themselves, which is really the point. (This kind of scheme could also be useful as a basis for family activities.)

Many family activities can be started now which may go on for years:

- Kite-flying and making.
- Fishing.
- Youth hostelling.
- Swimming, riding.
- Music.
- Writing and illustrating stories, making books.
- 'Adopting' people in need of help or company.
- Looking after animals.
- Cultivating an allotment.
- Cycling (if there's somewhere safe to do it).
- Indoor games-playing.
- Going to church or a similar organisation.

There are several more ideas in Chapter 13. If you are not in the habit of family activities now, it will be difficult to start them up when the children are teenagers. Obviously, many of these activities can be done in organised clubs. But although peer groups are important, they cannot replace the exchanges that take place between people of different ages and generations.

## FURTHER READING

See list on page 131 at the end of Chapter 8, much of which is relevant for this age group.

*Children Without Childhood*, Marie Winn, Penguin, London, 1983. Good as aversion therapy.

*The Education of the Child*, Rudolf Steiner, Rudolf Steiner Mail Order, 38 Museum Street, London WC1A 1LP, 01-242 4249

*Children's Minds*, Margaret Donaldson, Fontana, London, 1978. A classic. Very helpful, particularly if your child seems to have learning problems at school.

Books on specific topics or crafts in which the child is interested can be found in the library. If they do not have a children's book on the subject, a simple adult one would do if you can help with any difficulties.

The Brownies and Cubs are usually fairly easy to track down. If you are interested in the Woodcraft Folk, or in starting a Woodcraft group of your own, their address is The Woodcraft Folk, 13 Ritherdon Road, London SW17 8QE.

If you have a local Friends of the Earth branch you might be able to do something for the juniors (with their help). Otherwise you could start a Watch group (see page 195 for address).

# 11.
# PUTTING ENTERTAINMENT IN ITS PLACE

## THE NEED FOR ENTERTAINMENT

One of the consequences of the appearance of television sets in every living room (bar 2 per cent) and many kitchens, bedrooms and even bathrooms, in the land has been the fuelling by the entertainment industry of the modern expectation that passive, mindless entertainment is an integral part of daily life, both for adults and children. Whether or not one minds the children watching TV, or how much, is a minor issue compared with the conceptual shift that has taken place and the effect that this shift has had on children's lifestyles.

People have always wanted to be passively entertained from time to time. Primitive communities told each other stories round the evening fire, troubadours visited medieval courts, crowds flocked to public executions in the 17th century, and theatres have always drawn an audience. These and many other forms of entertainment have been sought out and enjoyed. Some of this entertainment has always been 'pure' entertainment, as far as we can tell, in the sense that it is a present experience that can be momentarily enjoyed and then forgotten, and some of it can more properly be described as 'art', in that it gives its audience a new perspective and an opening of mind and soul.

Most commercial entertainment does not set out to be art. Whether it be rock music on a personal stereo, video cartoons or quiz shows, it is a palliative, an easy way of temporarily anaesthetising oneself from daily life. This ability to escape from time to time can lend renewed vigour to the rest of life (just as a summer holiday, and even the promise of it, fortifies the rest of the year). However, the ability to escape from time to time is quite different, both conceptually and in its effects on the escaper, to the need for several hours of daily entertainment. If the escape from daily life becomes the part of the day most eagerly awaited, the quality of the rest of the day is in urgent need of assessment.

> Our age of agglutination has many unpleasant aspects: our environment is ugly and noisy, we are hurried and worried, people speak eagerly of 'getting away from it all' ... the extraordinarily high value which people set upon the vacation periods gives the measure of their discontent with their daily lives ... It is to the workaday world itself that pleasantness must be imparted.
>
> Bertrand de Jouvenel, from *Human Identity in the Urban Environment*

The entertainment industry is trying to impart pleasantness, and its mentality has invaded all realms of society. Matter-of-fact communications such as company reports to shareholders are dressed up and made to look like glossy magazines. Even museums are increasingly filled with exhibits designed to entertain. Many newspapers, and most commercially available magazines, aim to entertain far more than they inform or stimulate thought. Publishers of books find that they can sell a great many less serious new novels than they would like but that they can sell blockbusters – pure entertainment – by the million. Children's stationery – ordinary pencils and notebooks – is dressed up as 'Ghostbuster' packs. And the entertainer himself, the amusingly or effectively presented person, is increasingly becoming the only person of whom the general public takes any notice. Filmstars become presidents, writers of blockbuster novels become senior figures in political parties. However, this entertaining presentation does not actually make the content of the workaday world more pleasant; all it does is disguise it.

The amount of the world's resources consumed by entertainment and its side effects is massively out of proportion, for we do not need it all. Essentially, human beings are designed for activity, and the human spirit seems to be ennobled by action and activity. To be able to act reinforces the individual's sense of his own power, so he is less likely to be unhappy if he can do so. It is sometimes observed that volunteers in social work agencies, environmental groups or other voluntary organisations benefit from what they do at least as much as the people, animals or planet that they are trying to help. Which is a very good reason for helping; nobody loses. We all need to be needed and enjoy making significant improving contributions, however small. Indeed, one of the best cures for loneliness is not to try to get somebody to help, but to go and find a cause or person in need of help.

The more our lives are filled with entertainment, the less time there is available for achievement or contribution. For both children and adults, entertainment-filled time reduces the time available for play, for self-created entertainment, or for simply doing nothing.

## TRUSTING THE CHILD'S INNER RESOURCES

For years, child psychologists have suggested that the child deprived of adequate stimulation would be retarded in his development. Most of the children they studied before they drew this conclusion were those, for example in institutions, who were deprived as much of human contact as of material stimulation. However, their message has been translated both by sellers of toys and by baby-book writers into an implication that the child should never be bored. If this is believed, it becomes difficult to allow any kind of stillness or ruminative activity, because this often looks the same as boredom. (Adults are equally afraid of allowing each other to be bored; try sitting happily at a party watching everybody else and thinking your own thoughts, and you'll probably find that your host starts worrying that you are unhappy.) Because we are afraid that the child will be bored, rather than allowing him to learn to relieve his own boredom – if such it is – we are persuaded to buy toys, entertain him or sit him in front of the television. We do not trust him to find something from his own inner resources. And if we do not trust him to do so, he will learn not to trust himself, and he will be bored.

The children's entertainment industry is not confined to toys and television, although it is arguable that it has been stimulated by television. There is now quite a large number of live groups providing entertainments for children at weekends and during school holidays, and while some of these are quite fun, many of them are of very poor quality. Even much of children's television, which is said to be very good in Britain, talks down to children; presenters with inane grins on their faces and animals in clothes talking in stupid voices promote a certain kind of silliness which is really rather insulting to the dignity and the intellect of the children whose time it is filling.

Many children are actually deeply serious, but this is a characteristic of which adults appear to be afraid. The 20th-century idea is that what is enjoyable must be 'fun', and in an era in which appearances are often more important than content, people have to be seen to be enjoying themselves – which, on the whole, means having a bland television-presenter-style smile on their faces. Yet the play of children left to themselves, while clearly engaging and rewarding, often does not appear to be 'fun'; two three-year-olds will happily invent a game of mothers and fathers, doctors and nurses, shopkeepers and customers, and play for hours without so much as a grin. And yet what they are doing is entertainment – entertaining themselves. 'Fun' is only one possible kind of entertainment.

It is not actually necessary to spend large amounts of time entertaining children or having them entertained, and there are several reasons why it is undesirable. It takes away some of their own power; it removes them from local reality more than they need; and it actively encourages them not to be serious. If, instead of filling the bored child's time with entertainment, we ask him to tell us a story, or to stand on his head, or to finish making whatever he has not yet completed, this will cost us something – a little thought – but will give him the confidence to know that he can act upon his own situation (and ours, too, if he 'entertains' us). We could even suggest that he sit still and be bored for a few minutes, for then he will find out how ideas arise.

Fear of the child having unfilled time is a reflection of our own fears, particularly if we have only one child and we ourselves fear solitude. But the fear is unjustified. If the child has freedom and access to play materials, he will occupy himself, and as he gets older his ability to occupy himself will grow. He may go off and make a model. He may play imaginative games with whatever is at hand, like setting up his own school or surgery with a few dolls or soft toys. He may do something aimless, like hammering bits of old brick into sand. He may, if he has a garden, go and make mud pies or little ponds. He may read, or he may try out writing, or scribble. He might go and look in the garden, if he has one, for worms and spiders.

If there is more than one child, the possibilities are more than doubled. Two children or more together will quickly find them-selves playing hide and seek, or shops, or being drivers in traffic jams, or being policemen or pirates or animals. They may argue during their games, which might be offensive to some parents: television creates peace, assuming there is agreement on which channel to watch. But we should not fear arguments. To offer children palliatives instead is to deprive them of the experience of resolving differences and learning to compromise. It does not actually get to the root of the disagreement; it is parallel to taking pills for chronic headaches without finding out how to avoid the headache. Children need to play out their own dramas; their self-made entertainment can then perform the functions that art performs, of opening them up to new views and leading them to an increased repertoire of thoughts and feelings.

## IDEAS FOR DIY ENTERTAINMENT

Because the modern urban child is confined and cannot freely seek out company when he needs it, it is necessary to have some materials available for him to work with and some toys for him to play with, to help him entertain himself when he needs a palliative or wants to 'work' at his own activities. But there are times when he needs less entertainment than we imagine. One mother used to take books and toys to keep a child occupied in a doctor's waiting room, which looked directly out on to quite an interesting main road. One day she forgot to take the entertain-ments, so they started spotting cars and counting buses and making up stories about the people on the street. This one occasion convinced her that they were better off without the toys; that creating their own entertainment was both more enjoyable and more relevant to what they were doing and where they were.

The proliferation of commercially provided entertainment has begun to drive the old-fashioned notion of entertaining oneself, using a few simple materials, almost into oblivion. A pack of ordinary playing cards, for example, can provide hours of group or solitary entertainment. Many small children enjoy sorting them out, older ones may try to organise them more systematically. Children who are of an age to understand rules can start with a simple game of pelmanism (now called 'Memory' and sold in expensive boxed sets with picture cards), and to involve a whole family, any guests around and every ounce of mental effort and emotion, there is little to beat a game of racing demon (demon patience). This last game, as well as being great fun, also performs a number of educational functions, although that is hardly the point; it is good for hand-eye coordination, encourages alertness and scanning, is good for number recognition, and good for mental arithmetic on the scoring. It is also conceptually enlightening because each player needs to concentrate on his own activity while being aware of the whole process – but he does not need to know in detail what his neighbour is doing and will lose out if he tries to do him down. And all it needs is a few packs of cards and a table or floor (see page 185).

Games like Consequences (which smaller children can play as heads, bodies and legs) can be very funny, and only need scrap paper and pencils. And a good game of consequences can provide the basis for a new story, or a bit of home drama, or a puppet show.

Puppets are another medium with which members of a family or friends can create their own shows and entertain each other. Although a simple puppet theatre is not difficult to make out of wood or even cardboard cartons, it is not necessary to have anything as complicated or as permanent as this. Glove puppets, for example, or stick puppets, operated from below, can rise up from behind the back of a sofa. The very simplest puppets to make are probably stick puppets (see page 187). This kind of entertainment can be as simple or as complicated as the entertainers require – from one single puppet telling the audience what he has done all day, to a complicated plot with lighting effects, a taped or live soundtrack and props. Stick puppets have the virtue that they can be made with paper, glue, pencils and sticks almost anywhere; if you are on a wet holiday, for example, you could play out a holiday from indoors with the aid of stick puppets, and by the end of a wet fortnight you could end up with an epic drama. Or the children can make nursery rhyme or animal characters – they don't have to be works of art.

## PARTIES

The real party, with work preceding celebration, is becoming almost as much of a rarity as a plain game of cards. An increasingly common practice now among children going to play at each other's houses is to sit in front of a TV or video. Not only is this a part of everyday 'social' life, but it also extends to children's parties at which, rather than playing games or chatting with each other, the children are 'entertained'. Magicians and puppet shows have been a feature of the occasional children's party for years, but they are becoming a rule rather than an exception, and if a live entertainer is not available, a videotape replaces him. The modern entertainer is no longer surrounded by an aura of magic, either; he is quite obviously selling his services, and even the children know this. For at the end of the entertainment, the entertainer does his advertising; he gives the children his card (usually, as yet, without full details of his price, but that will surely soon appear) to 'give to Mummy and Daddy', who cannot then use the excuse to their own children that they do not know where to hire an entertainer.

It is not only the entertainer's card that the child takes home, but a plastic bag, often labelled 'Loot', containing various cheap and breakable items, usually ugly and sometimes unpleasantly noisy. Gone is the simplicity of a balloon and a piece of cake; a party is another stimulus to acquisitiveness. 'Where's my party bag?' is a not unusual question from a departing guest.

One puppeteer told me that she sometimes performs for the first hour of a party, and then her act is followed by children eating their tea out of boxes in front of a video. So a party, which once meant an occasion for communal play and a communal meal, is reduced to communal voyeurism and private eating.

Another form of party is a trip to the cinema and a visit to a hamburger bar (McDonalds do a special line in children's 'parties'). These are activities which most of the children would do anyway, are very expensive and are good for the environmentally damaging hamburger trade. It is difficult to resist children's requests for this kind of 'party', even if you want to and you know they would prefer a real party – unless there is an attractive alternative to hand.

Which there is – the children's party with games and a communal meal. Cheap, cheerful and fun. But it does take a couple of hours for parents and children to think it out and organise it. It is worth spending a few pounds on one of the party books on the market which contain ideas for games, food, etc. Fancy dress is one such idea, and here the eco-conscious has any number of themes that he could use, from birds, animals, flowers, jungles, to deserts. Ordinary party games can be varied around such themes; you can 'pin the tail on the parrot', 'hunt the daffodil bulb', have trays full of wildlife articles for Kim's game, in which you are shown a trayful of assorted items for a few minutes, and then when the tray is removed or covered up, you write down as many as you remember. The winner is the person or team who remembered the most. You can play musical and guessing 'Who am I?' animal games, and so on. Or you can, if you trust the weather, arrange to meet in a park, take a picnic there, and have an out-of-doors party. Going-home presents could be a packet of seeds, or a bulb (with instructions for growing them). Not only is this a lasting souvenir, but it is unifying for the children in January to be discussing the progress of the bulbs they were given at an autumn party.

## SELF-ENTERTAINMENT SKILLS FOR LIFE

Commercial entertainment is everywhere a part of life (it's almost impossible to find a cafe without background music, for example). The undesirability of this to the Green is not only its effect on the child's competences and in the waste of resources, but in the sense of values and lifestyle imparted by it. Not only does most entertainment tend to encourage a consumerist way of life, but, particularly in the case of television (because of the nature of the medium), it tends to be fast and fragmentary, a celebration of the superficial. Even the much-praised nature programmes can only show the dramatic; slow processes make boring television.

There are good programmes, and it may be thanks to television that the public, including children, is beginning to become aware of the problems that the planet is facing. (Ironically, it may well be a fixation on television that stops them doing anything about them; and the message is obscured when a good environmental programme about, say, the greenhouse effect is likely to be followed by an advertisement for a new fast car.) But too much TV viewing is obviously undesirable, and selectivity is crucial to its good use.

The same is true of pop music (some of which is quite pleasant) since the values imparted by many of the lyrics are often simply self-indulgent or self-seeking, and the dances that go with its often aggressive beat are private orgies. However, given that music and dance are ways in which the human being can participate in the rhythms of the universe, it is worth seeking out some of the alternatives, such as folk music and folk dance, whose rhythms and movements are less frenzied, even if equally obsessive. And if the words of a folk song make no sense to a child, they can make up some new ones.

Puppets, card games, etc., are activities which do not demand years of practice, although they may improve with it. There are, of course, various specialised activities which individual children enjoy, such as chess, sport or music, which need study and time but which will keep them in free self-entertainment for the rest of their lives, if they so choose. If a child is interested in one of these activities (and they are more likely to be if their parents are) it is worth encouraging them, since it will nourish them in several ways. Their interest may even lead the parents to become interested.

In this chapter I have emphasised the less studied entertainment possibilities for two reasons: firstly, they are available to everybody; and secondly, they give the whole family an opportunity to do something which is largely denied to adults after long years of schooling and work – the opportunity to look at the world and each other afresh through creating and playing together.

## FURTHER READING

*Human Identity in the Urban Environment*, G. Bell and J. Tyrwhitt, Penguin, London, 1972.

*Working at Leisure*, Barrie Sherman, Methuen, London, 1986. This is really almost a companion volume to Charles Handy's *The Future of Work*. It looks at global trends and raises new ideas for consideration.

*Amusing Ourselves to Death*, Neil Postman, Methuen, London, 1986. Not a long book, but none the less an in-depth analysis of how the entertainment mentality has invaded our lives and even the education system.

*Children's Parties*, Angela Hollest and Penelope Caine, Piatkus, Loughton, 1983. A practical helpful book with plenty of ideas about how to do your own party – planning, recipes, games, costumes, everything.

See also *Play*, on reading list for Chapter 6.

# 12.
# GREEN TEENS –
# THE AGE OF
# ADVENTURE

> Youth is the time to go flashing from one end of the world
> to the other both in mind and in body; to try the manners
> of different nations; to hear the chimes at midnight; to see
> sunrise in town and country; to be converted at a revival;
> to circumnavigate the metaphysics, write halting verses,
> run a mile to see a fire, and wait all day in the theatre to
> applaud 'Hernani'.
>
> R.L. Stevenson, *An Apology for Idlers*

And if the modern equivalents of these opportunities are
missing, they may be replaced by trips on LSD or crack, or
street fights, or watching video nasties, or sleeping around in
search of the most mind-blowing orgasm, or screaming frantic-
ally in a noisy concert. For the adolescent, the new owner of an
adult body and adult sexual feelings, is possessed also of a new
kind of energy which he needs to release. This often shows itself
as a form of impatience with his more pragmatic parents and
elders who are resigned to a reality which falls well short of the
ideals they cherished in their youth. He, however, cares about
issues with a passion and a perception which is all too often
suffocated in adults by the perceived burden of adult responsibilities.

## WHAT DO ADOLESCENTS WANT?

I vividly remember meeting for the first time a class of materially deprived inner-city 14-year-old girls, to whom I was

157

supposed to be teaching social studies, which was a new subject for them. I entered the room, we introduced ourselves and made ourselves comfortable round a large table. Before I had had the chance to speak, Lesley looked me straight in the eye and said 'Social studies! I suppose you're going to teach us about this bleeding rotten society and how we've got to fit into it.' I was silent for a moment, realising that the syllabus I had been given and had prepared fulfilled precisely those aims. It was going to be totally inappropriate to teach what I had prepared. These girls deserved more, and I was going to have to go away and rethink it all. Lesley, untrammelled by a teaching load, and unhampered by prejudices about what the subject should involve, was alive to the possibilities of the subject and its potential scope. What she and her friends wanted to do was to talk about society's values, how its institutions worked and why, and then see which parts of the system needed to be more fully understood in order that they could be changed. If I stopped Lesley from mentally flashing from one end of the world to the other, I could teach her for years and still she would not learn. Nor would I learn anything from her, and so all my teaching would be quite pointless.

This group, like most adolescents, wanted a structure and some help in ordering their thoughts and feelings. They did not want to skip off school, or destroy the world; they wanted the security of a teacher who was also a person who would help with the provision of limits appropriate to the shaping of their own ideas. Many adolescents want this at home too. While they are happy to be part of a cooperative, they will not willingly accept prescriptions. And there is little enough reason for them to do so – our generation's prescriptions for the world have caused at least as many problems as they have solved, and our children can see it. As adults, we have to be prepared to accept criticism of our many failures, while abiding by those of our principles we know to be right; we have to be prepared to discuss our failures and our principles with our adolescent children. And if we listen very carefully to them, and to what they want to tell us, we will hear of much that they have seen and that we haven't.

## THE ADOLESCENT IN SOCIETY

Adolescence is considered by many to be the most difficult stage of child-rearing, and yet very little help is offered to parents

Nearby, a just-born baby, with curly hair
and chocolate skin is opening his little
dark and weak arms and waving them as if imploring
the world to help him live his life.

You grown ups, we can't get dimples, as
you got when you were our age, because we
don't know how to smile, because we didn't
learn to smile. All we can learn is violence
and destruction. Grown ups we don't have
freckles on our face as you had, because ...
*you stole our sun!*
Olga Ciuperca (age 17), from *Cry for our Beautiful World*

compared with what is offered to mothers of tiny babies. This may be because hard and fast rules are considered inappropriate, for every family with adolescents tells a different story; or it may be because it is generally felt that parents cannot in any case control their teenagers, and many people do not buy advice unless it gives them definite solutions and, ultimately, some control.

The physical changes taking place during adolescence are at the root of many of the problems. We are, in western society, still pretty unhappy about admitting to the existence of basic bodily functions and to the idea that our bodies are living constantly-changing organisms. Shifts in hormonal proportions are one of these continuously changing determinants of how we feel and act. In the adult, these shifts may follow a regular cycle, perhaps monthly, and we learn to adjust to them. However, the hormonal changes taking place during adolescence signal a permanent change from childhood to adulthood and the need for the adolescent to grow into an adult identity. Yet our society does not find it easy to cater for the adult in each teenager. It does not, for reasons of their lesser experience, want teenagers to be classed as adults, and yet they are no longer children. A society which subdivides people into ages and stages as unequivocally as ours does has obvious problems when it can't quite define the correct roles for any one stage – so it has problems with its adolescents.

159

One resolution of this dilemma was made by youth itself in the creation of the so-called 'youth culture'. Initially this culture, with its symbols of pop stars, specific modes of dress, types of music and easily identifiable forms of behaviour, was created in the late 1950s by youth itself. But now it is no longer the creation of youth; many of those people who inaugurated it in the 1950s are now holding its purse-strings and are basically middle-aged entrepreneurs devising saleable forms of the culture. Even pop stars in their late 40s top the charts. This culture has been immensely powerful, for, despite adult dislike of adolescence, adults themselves are often striving to look and behave like teenagers. The word 'youthful' frequently appears in, for example, cosmetics advertisements. The notion that there might perhaps be age-appropriate appearances that are desirable, but unrelated to youth, is hard to find in any of the symbols of our culture.

Whether we like it or not, a youth culture is necessary in our present social structure, which debars teenagers from adult responsibilities which they might like to accept, and ensures that most of their time is spent absorbing large quantities of information in small rooms. They need to have an opportunity to work off their surplus energy, to take responsibilities and to assert their independence. These functions are performed to a certain extent by organisations such as the Scouts and Guides, but they are not as popular as they once were. There are youth clubs and interest groups of various different sorts, run by a number of agencies, but many of these are more aimed at entertainment than at fulfilling any particular ideals. The Friends of the Earth have just started up an environmentally directed youth section, Earth Action, for members of the 14–18 age group. This could provide ideals, responsibilities and the chance to take meaningful action. The opportunity to contribute practically and to campaign within a framework of specific socially oriented goals could help adolescents to identify possible aims for their own lives. Like the Scouts and other such youth groups, their aims are remote from the values currently presented by the adult media as being desirable – making money, looking 'good' (glamorous or smart), consuming conspicuously, being better than the next person in terms of worldly success.

Everybody needs to feel successful, and to have the importance of their contributions and achievements recognised. Unfortunately the possibilities of success available to the average adolescent in western society are largely confined to academic successes. Those who are most 'successful' are those who can compartmentalise mentally, putting aside their ideals for the duration of each school day, and plough their way along furrows of learning that have become virtually fossilised by the pressure of a million previous ploughs moving along the same track. If they keep to a straight line and report accurately on the state of the furrow, in an examination, they are deemed to have succeeded. Many of them, of course, fail. What those who succeed do not realise is that staying in the furrow can go on even until a youth has completed his doctorate – by which time he is hardly a youth and may not have a single original thought or idea left.

> The authors ... echo our own fears and experiences as Ph.D. students. A Ph.D. thesis seems meant solely to be a repository of unwieldy data – and data that conforms with the literature at that.
>
> Things are not very different at seminars. Research data are presented and a particular explanation is offered where two or more possibilities might coexist and they are all dismissed on the grounds that 'such examples are not found in the literature'.
>
> Letter to *Nature*, 27 April 1989

What is surprising, in view of the constant suppression of original ideas from young adults in favour of the status quo, is not that they are sometimes rebellious but that they are so patient. Their patience is partly due to perennial promises made of 'better things in a couple of years'. At about the age of 14, some subjects can be dropped at school and the student is left with his own 'choice'. If he is not allowed to do original work, he is told that the next set of exams will give him more scope – and the next, and the next. If, at home, he is also told that he can make his own choices only when he has left home, he will be doubly crushed. If his scope for both physical and mental adventure is thus limited, he is being deprived of the right to be who he is at his stage of the lifecycle. He is in no-man's land. It is small wonder that many adolescents become mildly depressed.

There are some schools which manage to avoid the worst excesses of the system, and individual teachers whose personality and enthusiasm genuinely fire their pupils, whose own interests they have at heart. But the education system is, generally speaking, not one in which teenagers are at their best. Parents have a major role to play, particularly with the teenager who does not fit in. For while they can encourage their children to make the most of those aspects of school in which they feel most comfortable, they can also explain the limitations of the system. If the adolescent understands that it is not a crime to be a misfit in a system, because the system itself is necessarily imperfect, he is automatically less of a failure. But it is vital that out-of-school activities, and life at home, should reinforce self-esteem. If he can't really adjust to school he can devote his passion and focus elsewhere. Sportspeople, craftspeople, musicians, members of active youth organisations, anybody with a serious interest, is well equipped. Many adults pursue this path, working their eight-hour day in order to fund their fishing trips, or kite-making clubs, or Greenpeace campaigns, or whatever they really care about which gives them meaning and status and inner satisfaction. The evening class is as much about living, in many cases, as it is about studying. Obviously this is not an ideal situation – it would be preferable if each individual could derive satisfaction from what he spent most time doing. However, these adolescents and adults are in a stronger position than those who are both bored at work and school and have no serious extra-mural interests; they are defended by their activities from the traps of the consumer rat-race, because their lives have meaning.

## HEALTHY FAMILIES

Obviously there are no rules about making life with adolescents easier, above and beyond the intent listening that makes life with anybody easier. It is, however, suggested by psychologists that families where there has always been good communication stand a better chance of a genuinely smooth passage without concealed tensions. An informal analysis of a number of families suggests that those who share common interests (these interests included art, science, tennis, music, walking, fishing) with their children, who are involved in groups bigger than the nuclear family, find life very enjoyable.

> Anyone who feels that they're in some way plugged into a
> meaningful, cosmic system is given a greater psychological
> balance as a result – whether or not they believe it contains
> a God-like figure at the control panel.
>
> Robin Skynner and John Cleese,
> *Families and How to Survive Them*

A study in Dallas found that 'the healthiest families seem to
subscribe to some transcendent value system, something beyond
themselves'. Many Greens feel plugged in, that they are related
to all other aspects of life on earth and that this massive global
family must be nurtured. This is the equivalent of a meaningful,
cosmic system. All actions have a meaning, and are not taken on
the basis of what seems convenient at the time.

When children become teenagers, and start seriously
developing ideals, they are fortunate if their parents still happen
to be idealistic. Here is common ground, the understanding of
idealism – even if the ideals are different, or if the parents have
thought through and rejected ideals which the teenager is now
pursuing. It can be quite tedious for ex-Marxists when their
teenage children discover Marx and start replaying arguments
that parents have long since rejected. There is no point in the
parents pretending they haven't heard the arguments before,
although, coming from a new person in a new context, there may
be interesting variations. But it is as rejecting to the adolescent
to say 'I know, I've been through all that' as it is to tell a new
Green that compost buckets are old hat. For the adolescent and
the new Green, these are new discoveries and should be
respected as such. And as they make these discoveries, the area
of common ground and common past experience is enlarged,
which itself makes communication easier.

Many teenagers appear to have no ideals. Many seem
demoralised, aggressive, angry, decadent. Those teenagers who
have ideals are, at school and outside, constantly being exposed
to and pulled by the others. Every teenager is a hair's breadth
from the drug culture, or a sexually transmitted disease, and
there cannot be a parent who has not felt some anxiety about the
possibility of her child getting mixed up with a harmful sub-

culture. The better the parent–child communication, the quicker the parent will sense the likelihood of actual danger and the more likely he is to be able to take some sort of averting action. For although parents may appear to have no control over adolescents, they have. Despite apparent rejection of adults and the need for independence, most adolescents want love and acceptance at home. If the home base is sound enough, the adolescent will see that the way that his own family approaches life provides a good basis for happiness and self-fulfilment.

## THE ACQUISITION OF LIFE SKILLS

Home has the responsibility for making sure that the teenager, when he or she decides to leave, is equipped with some basic life skills. The adult who cannot budget, who cannot cook and who cannot sew is an adult dependent on and at the mercy of others. Recent events illustrate this kind of helplessness. In April 1989 it was found that a number of jars of baby food had been contaminated with broken glass and other injurious materials by a group of blackmailers. This was reported on a Monday. On the subsequent Friday reports were still coming in of people who had gone on using these products, who had been unfortunate enough to buy contaminated jars and whose children were injured. Those who could sleep easily in their beds were those who could think of alternatives, and who found it little trouble to cook proper food instead.

The adult or student who can run his domestic life both cheaply and effortlessly, who is not forever muddling through chores, has a great deal of time and freedom available. But he is unlikely to find this easy if he has not been allowed some domestic and financial responsibility in his teens, because domestic skills need to be learnt. Budgeting his time is another art of a similar nature. Good organisation is worth learning early for the freedom it confers, and how much the teenager will learn that is of real use will depend on the orderliness of his home. Orderliness (which does not mean inflexibility) will in any case help the adolescent who may be suffering from inner disorder – he can do without being surrounded by outer chaos.

I kept just clear of going off the rails, which I nearly did a
number of times, because I liked my parents and I played
football. That gave me a chance to do something with lots
of adrenalin going, and to be an exhibitionist. It gave me a
great feeling. Without that I don't know where I'd have
ended up.

35-year-old builder

## GETTING HIS KICKS

From a basis of order, the adolescent can go off and find his
kicks, his heightened experiences, the modern equivalents of
those described by Stevenson. He needs these, and they will add
a new dimension to his outlook and personality. Some of them
can be got within the family, but not all.

Football can provide a high, and there are many other such
activities, some of which have already been mentioned. The
commercially sold kicks, such as bars, fashion, high speed motor
vehicles and drugs, however, receive a good deal more 'pushing'
than those which make nobody any money. But if the family
shares activities which include glimpses of life beyond the
ordinariness of daily life – activities which might include drama,
mountain walking, cooking inspired or exotic meals, cycling,
doing conservation work – their children may go on sharing
them as part of the family, or they may find peers with similar
Green interests. These activities will also discharge a great deal
of energy.

There are obvious problems in dealing with sexual energy.
This issue is fundamental to the whole of adolescence, and has,
in view of the AIDS crisis, been much written about. However,
most teenagers do not want to be drug addicts or TV junkies or
alcoholics, or catch sexually transmitted diseases, although
many see no alternative ways of having adventures.

## THE END OF ADOLESCENCE

He may leave home in his late teens, if he can find housing, or he
may stay. It may be considered rather odd if he actually wants
to carry on living with his family. In parallel with the toddler
who did not want to go to playgroup, something is thought to be

Family youth hostelling is an enjoyable and relatively cheap way of seeing a great variety of places. It is easy to plan; the YHA book gives addresses, telephone numbers and opening times of hostels. One can book by phone and confirm in writing; one can also pay in advance, although this is not essential. One can work out routes which tie in with public transport. It gives one a great sense of freedom not to be tied to a car, and to have several days in the open air completely away from roads, traffic and driving (the sense of well-being one gets from this cannot be over-emphasised). But there is no stigma attached to car-driving members. We started when our son was 11 and wished we had discovered family hostelling before. Since then our groups of 5–8 people have consisted of a mixture of adults over 40 and teenagers aged between 11 and 20. Our son, now 14, hopes to go on his own with friends this year … What appeals especially to the younger generation is the mixture of knowing roughly what to expect combined with the excitement of discovering what each new hostel is like.

Brigid Cherry

wrong if young adults do not leave, or do not want to leave. Obviously, since he is destined to set up his own home one day, he needs room for independent exploration outside his own four walls. But this is not the same as needing to leave. If each individual is allowed the mental and physical independence and privacy that he needs, and everybody is happy with the arrangement, it is pretty silly to split up a going concern for no very good reason.

He may, however, go not a moment too soon for all concerned, with everybody breathing sighs of relief. He may take on the values of the non-Green world and appear to become interested in personal aggrandisement at whatever cost. But often this change is temporary and experimental; research suggests that the values of early childhood eventually reassert themselves because the adult will never feel happy with himself if he rejects them totally. (He can be helped to reject them with therapy if there is an obvious need to do so.) Some reject them, but not many, and if those values and lifestyle gave him a strong sense of his own worth and of the joy to be found in nurturing and caring for his planet and the people on it, he will want to use his instincts to 'attend to the toilet of the planet' and to 'pull up the seedlings of the baobabs' whenever he sees them appear.

> Man is more greedy, selfish and thoughtless than ever before. Soon, if nothing is done, many will wish that they had never been born.
> Chidi Nwizu, age 14, from *Cry for our Beautiful World*

## FURTHER READING

*Understanding Child Development*, Sara Meadows, Hutchinson Educational, London, 1987. This is a guide to the whole of child development in our culture, with a good section on adolescence.

*A Parents' Guide to the Problems of Adolescence*, Penny Treadwell, Penguin, London, 1989. This is exactly what it says it is – how to deal with the problems, agencies which can help, what you can do about it.

*Families and How to Survive Them*, Robin Skynner and John Cleese, Methuen, London, 1983. This is about family relationships, and has a short but useful section on adolescents and what they need from their families.

*A Good Enough Parent*, Bruno Bettelheim, Pan, London, 1988.

*Cry For Our Beautiful World*, edited by Helen Exley, Exley Publications, London, 1985. This is an anthology of statements, poems and essays by children (mostly in their teens) about how they see the world and its future. These contributions are simple, passionate pieces on everything from the beauty of trees to the destructiveness of man. They could turn the hardest heart into a Green for the sake of the contributors.

*Blueprint for a Green Planet*, John Seymour and Herbert Girardet, Dorling Kindersley, London, 1987. Clear and beautifully illustrated book about most types of pollution – the causes, what can be done locally and globally. Good for most ages but specially suitable for the 10-14 age group.

# 13.
# IDEAS TO GET YOU STARTED

## BIRDS

There are many different birds that can be attracted to a garden
even in a town. Look at the list in the bird survey on page 173.
You may not know what all these birds look like and might need
to borrow or buy a book to help you to identify them – the
*Ladybird Book of Garden Birds* is a good one to use.

To persuade birds to come regularly to your garden you will
need to provide food, water and, if possible, nesting places. But
remember not to put food or water near undergrowth where the
birds could be ambushed by cats.

### Birdtables and feeders

You can buy birdtables and feeders, but there is really no need
to as they can be made cheaply at home. A table need be no
more than a flat piece of wood with narrow edges added, either
fixed on top of a post or hung from a bracket or tree branch. The
sizes given for the wood are just a guide – see what you already
have or can buy as off-cuts in a wood shop.

Table base $2\frac{1}{2}$cm $\times$ 30cm $\times$ 50cm, edges $2\frac{1}{2}$cm square.
Leave a gap at each corner for the rain to drain away. Try to
make the table large enough and the post high enough to make it
difficult for cats to reach. The table top can be fixed to the post
with either right-angle brackets or screwed through the table top
into the post.

Other feeders can be made from waste that you may have at
home; for example, a piece of wood (5 $\times$ 5cm or larger) as long
or as short as you like. You will need a brace and a bit to make
holes about $2\frac{1}{2}$–3cm diameter, 3–5cm deep. Perches will help
the larger birds; put small pieces of beading $2\frac{1}{2}$–5cm below
each hole. The holes should be filled with bird cake and the
wood hung on a nail in a post or a tree. Woodpeckers may be
attracted to this, as well as blue tits and great tits. Other birds

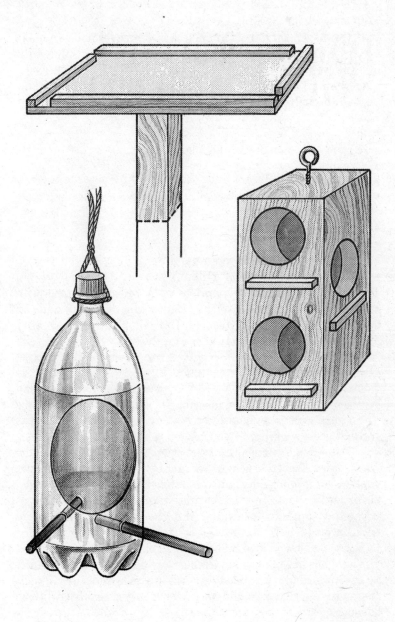

*Some easily made bird feeders*

such as blackbirds will try to use it but it will take them a little while to work out how to.

If you haven't the tools to make a wood feeder you can make very satisfactory feeders from plastic drinks bottles. Small birds like tits won't need perches, but larger birds will, so you could make two types. Perches can be made from narrow dowelling pushed through small holes just below the main hole.

## Food

Birds can be fed on any of the following:

- Peanuts – not salted.
- Wild bird seed.
- Sunflower seeds – these can be bought from a pet shop.
- Breadcrumbs – preferably brown.
- Oatmeal.
- Cooked rice.
- Dried and fresh fruit and nuts.
- Cheese, suet and bacon scraps.

These can be put out separately or a selection mixed with melted lard will make a bird cake (no cooking required) and can be put out in one of your feeders. But don't put nuts out after February – young birds may choke on them.

In the summer birds will find their own food, but don't forget to start feeding again in the autumn. In snowy or frosty weather you can help the birds if you turn over a small patch of ground for them to find worms and insects.

You can even grow your own bird food. Look to see what is growing in your garden if you have one – if the plants produce lots of seeds don't cut off all the dead flowers. Birds love the seeds from flowers such as poppies, evening primrose and sunflowers. If you have planted a butterfly garden leave the seed heads on the docks, nettles, thistles, dandelions and marigolds. If you buy sunflower seeds to feed to the birds you might like to try to grow a few. Soak the seed for a day or two then follow the seed sowing instructions in the gardening section below.

There are lots of shrubs with berries and fruit loved by birds; for example, holly, ivy, hawthorn, wild roses, cotoneaster, and of course the ones that you might like as well – raspberries, black-berries, cherries, plums, etc.

Water is essential to birds for drinking and bathing. You could provide it in a shallow plastic tray, like a cat litter tray, or in an upside down dustbin lid supported by bricks. An upside down flower pot with a branch in the hole then makes a good perch. You could also make a small pond in a sink.

*A bird water trough made from a dustbin lid*

## Nestboxes

These are easily made from wood. Make them as near as possible to the size given in the illustration, but use off-cuts of wood where you can. The simplest to make is an open fronted one. This will be used by robins, wagtails or wrens and should be tucked away in ivy, honeysuckle or a fairly thick bush if possible. The type with a hole in the front is for blue tits, great tits and perhaps nuthatches. These birds like their holes to be special sizes – 2.5 cm for blue tits, 2.8 cm for great tits and 3.2 cm for nuthatches. These boxes should be put in an open position but not where they will be in full sun in summer. Glue and then nail your box together using 1½ inch oval nails. One nest box can be made up from 5 feet of 6 in × ¾ in wood.

Other nest boxes can be made using plastic containers – experiment and see what works.

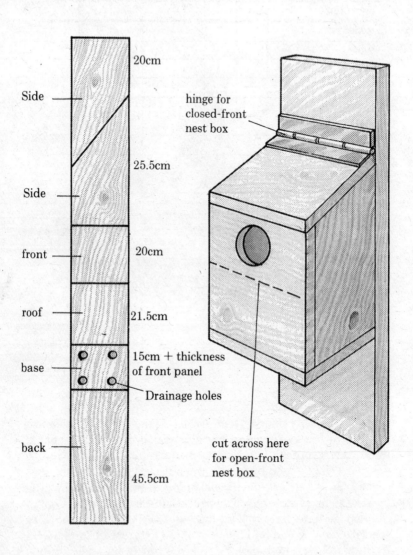

20cm

Side

25.5cm

Side

front — 20cm

roof — 21.5cm

base

15cm + thickness
of front panel

Drainage holes

back

45.5cm

hinge for
closed-front
nest box

cut across here
for open-front
nest box

*An easily made nesting box*

| DATE | | | | | | | |
|---|---|---|---|---|---|---|---|
| WEATHER | | | | | | | |
| BLUE TIT | | | | | | | |
| GREAT TIT | | | | | | | |
| LONGTAILED TIT | | | | | | | |
| GREENFINCH | | | | | | | |
| CHAFFINCH | | | | | | | |
| BULLFINCH | | | | | | | |
| BLACKBIRD | | | | | | | |
| ROBIN | | | | | | | |
| JAY | | | | | | | |
| MAGPIE | | | | | | | |
| SONG THRUSH | | | | | | | |
| STARLING | | | | | | | |
| BLACKCAP | | | | | | | |
| MISTLE THRUSH | | | | | | | |
| WREN | | | | | | | |
| SPARROW | | | | | | | |
| PIGEON | | | | | | | |
| HOUSE MARTIN | | | | | | | |
| SWIFT | | | | | | | |
| GREAT SPOTTED WOODPECKER | | | | | | | |
| FIELDFARE | | | | | | | |
| REDWING | | | | | | | |
| | | | | | | | |
| | | | | | | | |
| | | | | | | | |

SYMBOLS TO USE:

| | | | | |
|---|---|---|---|---|
| BIRD SEED | BS | SUN | ☆ |
| FLOWER HEADS | FH | CLOUD | ☁ |
| BERRIES | B | RAIN | /// |
| BIRD CAKE | BC | SNOW | ✳ |
| NUTS | N | | |
| INSECTS | I | | |
| FRUIT | F | | |

*Bird survey chart*

## Bird survey

All the birds listed in the accompanying bird survey chart on page 173 have been seen in city gardens. Fill in the date each time you survey the birds in your garden and draw in a weather symbol. Put a tick next to the name of the bird when you see it, or a food symbol if you can actually see what it is eating.

You will have to make the chart big enough to do surveys at different times of year, as some birds on the list only visit in winter and some only in summer. If you are lucky enough to see others not listed, you will have to make an extension to your survey. And obviously, if you live in the country your list can include other birds.

## BUTTERFLIES

There are about 70 different kinds of butterfly in this country. Illustrated on page 176 are five of the more common butterflies you might find in your garden. There will be others if you live near parks or woods and if you grow the right plants. The *Ladybird Book of Butterflies and Moths* is helpful in identifying the butterflies, as is Usborne's *Butterflies*.

There are four stages in the lifecycle of a butterfly – the egg, which hatches into a caterpillar, which becomes a chrysalis, from which the butterfly emerges. All of these can be found or spotted.

## Plants to attract butterflies

To attract butterflies into your garden, you need:
- Nectar plants – these provide the flowers from which the butterfly feeds.
- Food plants, on which the butterfly will lay its eggs and which the caterpillar will eat.

Butterflies are very particular about where they lay their eggs, and most use only one or perhaps two or three types of plant for their eggs, but they all use many different nectar plants.

There are probably nectar plants growing in your garden already; for example, sweet William, Shasta daisy, Michaelmas daisy, polyanthus, phlox, golden rod, honesty, wallflowers and buddleia (the 'butterfly' bush). These are all plants that will not flower the same year that you sow the seed, but marigolds, alyssum, petunias and tobacco are some of the annual flowers liked by butterflies that can be sown in spring to flower in the summer. You can also buy strips of these plants fairly cheaply from a garden centre. If you have pots of polyanthus indoors, these can be planted outside when they have finished flowering.

The food plants that may grow in your garden are probably pulled up as weeds; these include stinging nettles, dock, couch and other meadow grasses, white clover and thistles. Try to have these weeds in the butterfly garden. There are also useful nectar weeds, including dandelion and red and white dead nettle; these are good for bees, too, as they flower early in the year when bees have few flowers to feed from.

Here is a list of a few types of butterflies and the food plants they need for their eggs.

| | |
|---|---|
| • Peacock | Stinging nettles |
| • Small tortoiseshell, red admiral, common blue | birds foot trefoil |
| • Large white | nasturtium |
| • Small white | cabbage |
| • Comma | wild hop |
| • Skippers (large and small) | grasses |
| • Small copper | dock and sorrel |
| • Browns, hedge, wall and meadow | grasses |
| • Holly blue | holly and ivy |

## A butterfly garden

If there is space in your garden you could plant a butterfly garden using most of these food plants and the nectar plants. However even a sink, tub or window box would provide enough space for a small garden. Use some stinging nettles (wear rubber gloves when transplanting these), docks and grasses. To prevent the roots spreading, plant these in old paint or syrup tins sunk into the soil, but do not use tins that have been opened with a tin opener. Then add some of the prettier flowering plants, e.g. polyanthus and marigolds, and the nectar weeds – dandelions and dead nettles. If you don't have any of these weeds/wild flowers in your garden, or don't have a garden, ask somebody with a garden or allotment if they would save you some of their weeds; the Ladybird Book of British Wildflowers will help to identify the plants you need.

There are many unworked plots of garden and land in cities. If you can find the owner, he may be happy to let you work the piece of land. Old people often find they have more garden than they can cope with, and like company. And if you would like to

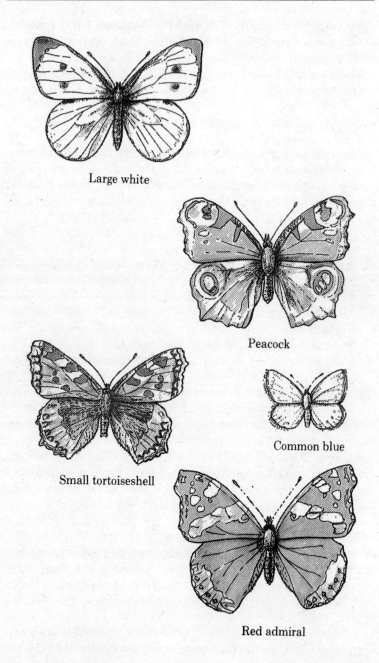

Large white

Peacock

Small tortoiseshell

Common blue

Red admiral

*Some common garden butterflies*

grow some wild plants for butterflies you can get a catalogue from John Chambers, 15 Westleigh Road, Barton Seagrave, Kettering, Northants. They also sell plants and bulbs. You should enclose a stamped addressed envelope, at least A3 size, for your reply.

## INDOOR GARDENING

Indoor gardening is obviously more limited than outdoor gardening and there are quite a lot of things that cannot be grown at all indoors. The ideas here are for things that can either be grown completely indoors, or started off inside (like seeds for the garden). Most of these ideas can be considered if you have a well-lit windowsill, and if you can find a light, warm, slightly moist environment most things are possible.

It is best to use a bought compost. Any of the usual brands of soil or peat-based composts are suitable for the ideas that use soil; peat-based are more expensive and are hard to water properly but are lighter to carry. Plastic pots don't break as easily as earthenware ones although they are ecologically less desirable, and yoghurt pots with holes bashed in the bottom are particularly good (wash them first). Table forks and spoons are good for handling seedlings. A small watering-can is useful, as are labels, although they fall off when wet; it is worth labelling the pots with a waterproof pen or chinagraph wax pencil.

Watering from underneath is best, because soil erosion can be caused by watering from above. Lower the container into a bucket or washing-up bowl of (not too cold) water until the water is level with the soil in the pot. Count slowly to ten, and put it somewhere (not straight down on the table) to drain. Water whenever the surface of the soil is dry to the touch.

### Mustard and cress
Sow the seed on 1 cm depth of thoroughly moistened peat-based compost. Deep-sided containers are best. Keep it dark, warm and moist for three to four days. When the leaves are level with the top of the tub give them moderate light so they become green.

Plain white mustard is the fastest; cress is slower to germinate and needs sowing three days sooner than mustard. Sow it very thickly. It's very nice in salads and sandwiches, and as decoration for savoury food. For fun, try sowing the seeds carefully on cloth to form numbers or letters (for birthdays?) or on top of a paper face to form hair.

## Sprouting seeds

Almost any seed will produce an edible sprout, but mung, aduki, fenugreek, alfalfa, green lentils, soya bean and chick peas are probably the nicest sprouts to eat. Never use seeds other than those meant for cooking or sprouting because seeds for sowing are often treated with fungicides and other chemicals. And don't use castor beans or red kidney beans.

You need a wide-necked jar (coffee jars are good), a piece of muslin to cover its mouth and an elastic band to keep it there. Put a teaspoonful of small seed (alfalfa), a dessertspoonful of middle-sized seed (fenugreek, mung, aduki or lentils) and a tablespoon of large ones (soya, chickpeas) to each half-pint size of jar. Cover with muslin and pour in enough warm water to cover the seed. Stand the jar overnight and drain off. Rinse and repeat this twice daily, keeping the jar in a dark place and on its side between rinsings. Sprouts should be ready to eat in a few days. (They will not look like the long straight ones that supermarkets sell, but will taste much better.)

## Sowing seeds in general

Large seed, i.e. those you can pick up one at a time, can be sown individually in pots. Fill the pot, tapping it to settle the soil but not packing it tight, and then simply poke the seed into it. Or you can make a hole with a pencil and drop it in. Cover with soil, and water from above. Don't forget, the soil will settle further, so do not underfill the pot.

With small seed, i.e. those you can see easily but can only pick up one by one with difficulty, fill a seed tray (or margarine tub) with soil so that it's much too full all over, scrape the excess off the top with the side of a ruler and firm the soil gently by pressing it down with a piece of cardboard. Scatter the seed evenly over the surface, cover the seed with a depth of soil equal to the diameter of the seed, level it with the ruler and firm it gently again. Water from above with a fine 'rose' or spray, very delicately so you don't splash the seeds out. Put it in a warm place out of direct sunshine, cover with plastic and newspaper (or put it in an old plastic carrier bag). Check every day and, when the seeds have germinated, remove the covering and bring them into more light (but not too much).

When they are bigger the seedlings can be put into pots (like holed yoghurt pots) one or two at a time. This needs to be done very carefully. Put some soil in the pot, and loosen the seedling's roots by running a spoon handle round the edge of the soil. Shake the container a bit to loosen further. It is important not to break the roots. Now make a hole in the soil in the pot with the blunt end of a pencil, pick a seedling up very carefully by its leaves (not its stem), lower it in and firm the soil around it. You may want to keep these plants in pots or plant them in the garden. Never give them very hot direct light, and do not keep them wetter than damp.

There are lots of different kinds of plants that can be grown indoors, and very many that are best started indoors before being planted outside (for more detailed instructions than given here, look for a simple gardening book). One of the best food plants to grow indoors is tomatoes, which are also very attractive plants. Some of the best flowers, which have large seeds, grow fast, are not too fussy and flower for a long time, even in pots, are sweet peas, ten-week stocks, calendula, French and African marigolds, tagetes, cornflower and candytuft. If you want to plant these out in the garden, wait until all danger of frost is past. The same thing applies if you want to plant them in window-boxes outside; window-boxes look good, are fun to look after and give a bit of extra garden space.

## Bulbs

These are ideal for indoor gardening. Cover them with soil in their pots, put them in a cool(ish) dark place (we use a corner of a toy cupboard) and keep them damp. When there is about 3 cm of stem showing, bring them into the light.

## Trees

Trees, as you will know, are extremely important for preserving the balance of nature, so see if you can start growing them.

The trees can be started in pots at home, then moved on to a tree nursery on an outside patch of land, and finally planted out to make a tiny wood.

Many trees are hard to grow, but if you sow acorns or sweet chestnuts as soon as they drop in autumn they will germinate straight away. You can grow them in pots in or out of doors. If you and your friends can grow some, you may then be able to persuade your local authority to let you have an area where you can plant a coppice in a few years when the seedlings are big enough. You could write to the authority and ask them for their reaction.

## Fun plants

Cut the tops off carrots or pineapples and put them cut surface down in a saucer of water. They won't produce fruit, but look lovely – carrot 'ferns' can be used in flower arrangements. Or try building miniature gardens using gravel and sand, with carrot, parsnip and beetroot tops. Or you can cut off the top, scoop out the root so you can get the top joint of your thumb into it, thread a piece of cotton through it so it will hang upside down and then fill the cavity with water.

## GARDENING

The fresh fruit and vegetables we grow play a very important part in the health and well-being of our children. Possibly within the next few years it could be the only source of affordable chemical-free food, unless organic food prices fall. So it's important to encourage our children to take a more active interest and learn the values of naturally grown food – values which will serve not only them but their own children.

One way to capture children's interest is to start by discussing their favourite fruit and veg. Then set about planning together what should be grown and the best way to grow it (you will find books in your local library). A good seed catalogue is helpful and it will show the plants to be grown.

Make sure that they can have a little plot of their own where they can experiment – they may have to be allowed to make some mistakes. Tell them about the different plant values. Encourage them to grow herbs – rosemary, sage, chive and mint are easy to grow and are very attractive plants.

Be careful with sharp tools. Children have to learn to handle them wisely, especially deceptive tools like garden forks which are much more dangerous than they seem. Try to buy a 'lady's' fork and spade for the children to use (and for you when you don't want to manhandle huge quantities of soil).

If you are on an allotment, there is plenty of wildlife to look at as well as what is being grown – usually birds, butterflies, insects and wild flowers. They are very pleasant places in which to spend time and you can keep a few things to do in your shed or

store cupboard there if your children become bored with
gardening. Keep drinks available in your shed, and maybe
something to eat. Children revive very quickly with these,
specially if the weather is either very hot or very cold.

If you can get an allotment but haven't much time to spend
on it, don't try to grow plants which need a great deal of care
and attention. Keep it simple and you will avoid frustration and
failure. As you and your children acquire more expertise, you
will be able to branch out.

To get an allotment, ring your local council, and ask for
whoever is responsible – there may be a waiting list, but keep on
trying. Working an allotment is a great way of spending productive, purposeful time in the open air, and is especially worthwhile if you have no garden at home. Tilling the soil is an
experience that keeps one really in touch with natural cycles.


## COOKERY

We are becoming increasingly reliant on prepackaged foods from
the supermarket; many of these foods contain ingredients that
may not be good for us. It is therefore important that children
learn to cook early and to use their imagination in developing
their own recipes if they have the chance. The following recipes,
which can be made by very young children (if they can read,
they could copy down a basic recipe into a scrapbook and then
add their own variations), can be varied almost infinitely. They
are listed in age order – the first ones can be made by very young
children, while the later ones are more suitable for older
children. All these recipes provide much scope for variation and
development.

### Fruit salad
Take one apple, one pear, one banana and one orange. Wash the
apple and pear (if they are not organic they will have been
heavily sprayed). Peel the orange and banana. Chop all the fruit
into small pieces – pretty shapes if you like, as a fruit salad does
not need to be all cubes – and put it in a bowl. Sprinkle a
spoonful of sugar or honey over the fruit and stir it. Then leave it
for an hour or two, covered with a plate (there is never any
reason to use clingfilm) for the flavour to develop. Serves three;
you can serve it with yoghurt or cream.

This basic recipe can be varied by using other fruits, by

adding other fruits or by using entirely different fruits. You could add lemon juice, which helps to bring out the flavour. If you are using red berry fruits, a little concentrated apple or blackcurrant juice gives a good flavour. You could make a 'shaped' fruit salad, by using melon, apple and pear all cut into diamonds or triangles. You can make fruit salad jelly. But do be careful to wash all fruit that is not going to be peeled.

## Sandwiches

Made with good bread and filling, these can be as nourishing as a cooked meal. Butter some slices of bread. Find your filling – perhaps sliced cheese or hard-boiled eggs mashed or sliced, with cress, sliced tomato, lettuce or cucumber. Put the filling on one slice of buttered bread. Put another slice of bread on top, butter side down, and press hard so the filling is secure. Cut into halves, quarters or triangles.

## Salads

Most vegetables are good in salads. Like fruit, they need to be washed before use. Try, for starters, chopped beetroot mixed with chopped celery and chopped apples. Or sliced cucumbers mixed with sliced tomatoes. (Sprinkling a little sea salt on salads helps to bring the flavour out, but don't use too much.) Grated carrot mixed with grated beetroot is tasty and colourful, but make sure the children understand how to use the grater safely. Radishes can be cut into pretty shapes, and look nice on a bed of cress (which the children can grow – see page 177).

If children serve a salad with wholemeal bread and cheese, they can present a complete, nourishing meal by the time they are about six, and there's not a lot of washing up.

## Simple buns

This basic bun recipe makes 12 buns/small cakes in patty tins. You need weighing scales, a mixing bowl, small bowls to put ingredients in, patty tins, and a large wooden spoon for mixing.

Measure out 125 grams (4 oz) each of margarine, brown sugar and wholemeal flour (self-raising, or add baking powder to plain flour). You will also need two eggs. Put the sugar and margarine in a mixing bowl and beat until they are creamy and well mixed. Add a dessertspoon of flour and one egg; mix in really well. Then add a bit more flour and the other egg. Mix again. Then add the rest of the flour and mix in well, until the mixture feels a bit like mud. (If it is too stiff you might have to add a spoonful or two of milk or yoghurt or fruit juice.) Grease and flour the patty tins, spoon the mixture into them, and cook in an oven preheated to 375 °F, 190 °C, gas mark 5, for about 20 minutes. Get them out, let them cool in the tins for a couple of minutes and then turn them out on to a wire rack to cool. Make sure you use an oven cloth to hold the tin and a cloth for the buns to prevent burning.

This is a basic recipe; if you want to turn it into small chocolate cakes, add a tablespoonful of cocoa when you are adding the eggs. If you want them to taste orangey or lemony, add the graded rind and juice of a lemon or orange. Or you could add half a cupful of sultanas or other dried fruit, which can be presoaked if you want to vary the texture. You could make icing and ice them when they are cool. Once you have got the hang of the basic recipe there are lots of ways you can vary it; start by trying to vary the proportions of the ingredients, which will produce different textured cakes.

## Chocolate kisses

You need 125 grams (4 oz) butter or marge, 50 g (just under 2 oz) caster sugar or soft brown sugar, 125 grams of self-raising flour and 25 grams (1 oz) of cocoa powder.

Beat the marge and sugar until light and creamy. Mix the flour and cocoa in very thoroughly. Grease a couple of large flat baking trays (and flour them). Wash your hands, make the mixture into walnut-sized balls, put them on the baking trays and flatten them with a damp fork. Bake them in an oven gas mark 5 (375 ° F, 190 °C) for 10–15 minutes. Makes about 20.

This basic biscuit recipe can be varied, just like the buns; try, instead of cocoa, desiccated coconut or ground almonds; or sultanas, or carob powder, or orange and lemon rind grated.

Economy note: It is pretty wasteful of fuel to heat up the oven to cook a single item, so try to do several things at one time.

## Plain lentil pudding

Take a cupful of lentils, one onion and two carrots chopped very fine, and a handful of parsley washed and chopped very fine. Wash the lentils in a sieve, picking out any stones or bad bits. Then put them in a saucepan with two and a half cupfuls of water, the onion and the carrot. (It adds to the flavour if you crumble a stock cube in at this stage.) Cook them, with a lid on, bringing them to the boil and then simmer slowly until you have a soft mush (20–40 minutes). Check occasionally to make sure the contents of the pan are not getting dry; if they are, add more water. If you add lots of water and a little salt and pepper, and then mash or liquidise this mixture, it makes good soup. You can add any other vegetables you happen to have around, too.

If you make the mixture very thick you can wait for it to cool down a bit, then beat in an egg and mix in the parsley. Then you can either put the mixture into a loaf tin (or cake tin), well greased, and cook it in the oven for about 45 minutes at 190 °C, 375 °F, gas mark 5, to make a sliceable lentil loaf, or you can shape it into balls, flatten them into round shapes and fry them as rissoles.

Any number of variations and additions of herbs, spices, vegetables, etc., are possible with this recipe. It serves about four for a main course, and green salad goes well with any of the versions, either hot or cold.

## Bread and butter pudding

This is a good way of using up slightly stale bread (if you haven't used it all for feeding the birds). It is delicious and much lighter to eat than you might expect. This recipe serves four people.

You need four buttered slices of bread from a large loaf, one tablespoon of sultanas, two rounded tablespoons of sugar, two eggs, ½ pint of milk, a few drops of vanilla essence and a 1½ pint pie dish.

Butter the inside of the dish. Press the slices of bread together in pairs to make two sandwiches, trim away the crusts and then cut each sandwich into about six cubes. Turn on the oven to gas mark 5 (375 °F, 190 °C). Place the bread in the pie dish and sprinkle with the sultanas and sugar. Crack the eggs into a bowl and add the milk and vanilla essence; whisk very thoroughly and then pour the mixture over the bread. Let the pudding stand for 15 minutes for the bread to soak. Place the dish in the oven and bake for 35–40 minutes or until the pudding is risen, firm and golden brown. Serve with cream or yoghurt or stewed fruit or on its own.

Variations: savoury, with cheese instead of sugar; any kind of dried fruit or nut; lemon, orange or coffee added; a thin layer of sliced fruit at the bottom of the bowl; etc.

## HOW TO PLAY RACING DEMON

You need a reasonable sized table, and one pack of cards per person, each with a different design on the back.

To start with, each player puts down his demon next to him; this is a pile of 13 cards face down, except for the top one which is face up. Then he puts four further cards face up in a row in front of him. The aim of the game is to get rid of the demon. His bit of the table will look like the illustration on page 186.

When play starts, each player turns over his cards, in threes, in front of him. If he gets an ace (or if he has one on any of his five original face-up cards) he must put it in the middle of the table, where everybody can reach it. Other players (or the same one) then add cards in sequence to build up this same suit on its ace. They may take these cards either off the top of the demon, from the four face-ups, or from what they turn up as they go through their hand. Every time a card is taken from the four face-ups, the player replaces it from the top card of his demon, immediately turning the next one face up. Each player may also build downwards in alternate colours on his four face-ups, e.g. put a red 9 on a black 10, then a black 8, etc. This gets rid of his cards and may help reduce his demon. However, only the bottom card on these piles may be removed to add to the common piles in the middle.

If a suit in the middle is finished, with a king on top, whoever finished it removes it from the centre and puts it beside him. Play stops when the first player to get rid of her demon shouts 'Out'.

Scoring: each player gets one point for each card on the common piles (they all have to be sorted out first). Each player loses two for each remaining card in her demon. Anybody who completed a suit in the middle gets an extra two points. After each round, each player shuffles her cards, cuts with the next door player, and the pack moves on to the next person. The scoring is cumulative; and fortunes can change very quickly – you can go from minus 7 to +15 in one go if you happen to go out quickly.

Obviously, the scoring can be varied. You may not like to score at all, just to try to get out (particularly with under-sevens). You can add or subtract different amounts, e.g. only lose one for each card in the demon, or add five for a suit completed. You could handicap so that the player who gets out first has to add an extra card to his demon, or the one who has

A. A different pack
   of cards per
   player

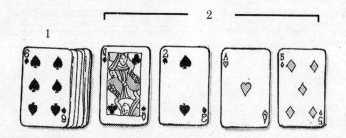

B. One player's demon
   at start of play:

   1. 12 cards face down,
      13th face up on top
   2. 4 cards, face up
   3. Rest of the pack,
      face down at start.

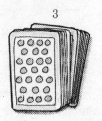

*How to play racing demon*

most left subtracts one. Variations such as these can be invented to fit the ages and skills of the players. There are no hard and fast rules to any private game, but all players must know the rules that are being played in advance, to avoid argument. Jot down the variations you have agreed before you start.

## STICK PUPPETS

To make stick puppets all you need is a pencil and paper (A3 size cartridge paper is ideal, as it needs to be quite stiff, but you can use any old plain thin card or other paper – this is a variable recipe). You need sticks – green garden canes, about 18 inches long, are ideal. Newspaper rolled up very tightly also makes sticks. Again these can be variable.

Cut a long rectangle of paper; fold it in half and draw the character you want. If you make him go right up to the fold it makes life simple. Then holding the paper so that it is like a closed card, cut round your shape; if the character goes to the top there will be a fold there.

Draw the back of the character. Any colouring, detail, etc., is best done at this stage. Then gum or paste the insides of the character and fold them down on to the stick; in the illustration the stick is the dotted line, which acts as the man's spine. The puppets are operated from below.

Variations: you can do similar things with horizontal sticks and operate the puppets from the side. If you want groups of people or animals, you can draw the group and operate it on one stick (perhaps a family of rabbits, or inseparable twins). You can make props with pieces of folded paper which can be propped up on the sofa back, if that is what you are using. Or make a theatre for them. When not in use, the puppets look good put in a vase, a bit like a bunch of flowers – and it keeps them in a state of good repair.

## MAKING RECYCLED PAPER

This is (or can be) a bit messy, so make sure you are working somewhere which is easy to wipe clean.

You will need old newspaper, a piece of wire mesh (about 30 cm square would be a good size to start with, obtained from a garden centre or hardware store), some absorbent cloths, e.g. old tea towels, two buckets or large bowls, a wooden spoon or

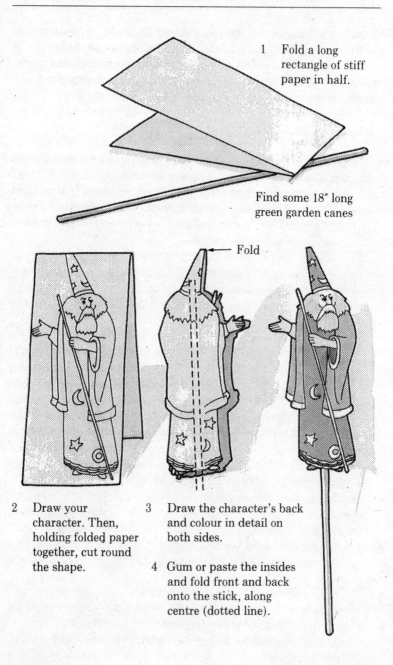

1 Fold a long
rectangle of stiff
paper in half.

Find some 18″ long
green garden canes

Fold

2 Draw your
character. Then,
holding folded paper
together, cut round
the shape.

3 Draw the character's back
and colour in detail on
both sides.

4 Gum or paste the insides
and fold front and back
onto the stick, along
centre (dotted line).

*How to make stick puppets*

liquidiser, powder paint (to make coloured paper), a plastic bag and some weights – heavy books, bricks or stones would do.

Soak some old newspaper in a bucket overnight. The next day, drain off the surplus water. Mash the paper and water into a pulp, using either the wooden spoon (lots of work, good exercise), the liquidiser or a Mouli-grater. Mix in some paint if you want the paper coloured.

Lie a cloth down flat on a clean, flat surface such as a board or a tray. Slide the wire mesh into the pulp mixture, and lie it, pulp side down, on the cloth. Press it down hard, then peel off the mesh, leaving the pulp on the cloth. Put another cloth on top and press down firmly. Repeat this process with the rest of the pulp and cloths. When you have used it up, put the plastic bag on top and weight the pile down.

After several hours (or overnight) the pulp will have turned to paper. Gently peel the paper off the cloths, and leave them on some newspaper to dry out completely. Then the paper is ready for use. If you have not got old absorbent cloths, tea towels are perfectly washable and usable after they have been used to make paper.

If you get good at this, you can use big bits of mesh and then cut up the paper to the size you want. Obviously the paper will never be white – but we have to get used to off-white things anyway because so much chlorine is used in getting them white and this is not very beneficial either to us or to the environment.

And there are other ways of re-using paper:

- Paper that is only used on one side can be made into telephone and shopping list pads very easily – just cut it into lots of same-size strips and sew or staple them at the top.
- Wrapping paper from presents, if removed carefully, can be used over and over again. It sometimes improves if it is ironed with a cool iron.
- Envelopes can be reused if carefully opened; re-use labels can be bought from Oxfam, Friends of the Earth and other organisations.
- Try to find a recycling scheme which will take your old newspapers.
- Use strips of damp newspaper as a mulch in the garden.
- Don't have bonfires if you can avoid it; it is better to recycle than to burn.
- Try to persuade your fish and chip shop to use newspaper instead of plastic bags.

## BAGS

Most of us use plastic carrier bags for shopping. You could get your children to count how many come into your house in one week. Even if they are kept for re-use, they are usually thrown away after a very short while. No plastic bag is biodegradable (even those that say they are only disintegrate, leaving a residue of plastic in the soil) so they cannot be recycled easily. It makes more sense to use fabric bags that can last a long time, and which will carry a greater weight without breaking.

Here are instructions for a simple shopping bag. It can be made by hand, but would take rather a long time. If you use a sewing machine you can add material to the top of the bag to strengthen it.

All that is needed is a rectangle of material 1 metre by ½ metre. The best material to use is cotton or a cotton/polyester mix; if you would like the bag to be waterproof use vinyl, a plasticised cotton. Look out for suitable material at jumble sales – skirts, dresses or sheets for example – but make sure that it is in good condition or it will tear. You could buy new material; apron cloth is very strong and comes in just the right width. You can use the same material for the handles but it would be better to buy webbing. For handles only you will need 1 metre and for handles and to strengthen the top you will need about 2 metres.

Fold the material in half to make a ½ metre square. The fold is the bottom of the bag. Sew up the side seams using a back stitch or sewing machine. Now turn right side out. Push the bottom fold up inside the bag 7 cm, then overstitch the sides using backstitch again to hold the folded material in place.

You will have to turn in a hem at the top of the bag unless you have a selvage (a finished edge on the material); turn in the hem before sewing on the handles. For the handles cut two pieces of webbing each ¼ metre long. Stitch these handles to the outside of the top edge. Using a sewing machine stitch the extra webbing around the top outside edge (if you are hand sewing your bag you may prefer not to do this part).

Once your bag is made you can draw on it; fabric crayons are good for this and easy to use. If you have used a patterned material draw a design or slogan on plain material and stitch it on to the bag. You might put 'Try a real bag – it saves on plastic' or a bird or a logo that you like.

Other bags that are easy to make include:

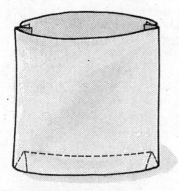

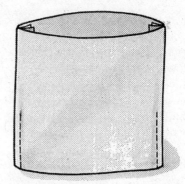

Sew up the side seams. Push the bottom fold up inside the bag 7cm.

Overstich the edges (just bottom 10cm if hand-sewing)

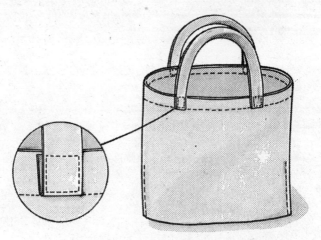

Turn in a hem on top edge. Stitch webbing handles to outside of top edge. Finish top outside edge with webbing.

*How to make a simple bag*

- Cloth bags – children can make them for their PE clothes or library books. If they like doing it, they are good to make as presents or for sale at fund-raising events.
- If you and the children enjoy sewing, try a patchwork bag – sew rectangles or diamonds of different colours and patterns together until there is enough to make up the bag.
- Shoulder bag – has longer handles and a narrower width than the standard bag.
- Drawstring bag – a long lace threaded through a $2\frac{1}{2}$cm hem at the top of the bag.
- Duffle bag – handles sewn top to bottom of a drawstring bag.

Apron cloth is available from John Lewis, 115 cm wide, bleached white, but is cheaper from Limericks Linens Ltd, 117 Victoria Avenue, Southend-on-Sea, Essex SS2 6EL, although you need to pay postage. Limerick's have unbleached cloth as well as bleached, 91 cm wide – about the right width for a bag. They will send you a free catalogue.

## FAMILY ACTION TO REDUCE POLLUTION AND THE GREENHOUSE EFFECT

- Use less paper. Look at rubbish thrown away at home/school. Can any of it be re-used? Can any of it be recycled? Take glass to a bottle bank. Take tins to save-a-can. Try and find somewhere to take paper. Food waste can be composted.
- Save energy. In cold weather keep the cold out, shut doors, etc. Switch off lights, etc., when not needed. Wear more clothes instead of turning the heating up. Do active things that warm you up and keep you fit.
- Do not buy or use products with CFCs in them.
- Hand-weed the garden instead of using chemicals. Plastic bottles cut in half keep slugs off plants, or (contact the Henry Doubleday Association) there is a poison which kills slugs but not the birds which eat them.
- Re-use plastic bags, which can be washed between uses.
- Buy or make a shopping bag and use it instead of plastic carrier bags. This saves lots of plastic – and won't break on the way home.
- Do not accept additional bags for things already wrapped.
- Try to use the car as little as possible, so that children get

used to using their legs/bikes or public transport. In any case, have the car converted to run on unleaded petrol if that is possible.

- Plant trees, which are life-sustainers, and look after existing ones.
- Try not to burn rubbish – compost and recycle wherever possible.
- Try to keep informed about what is going on.
- Tell your friends about what is going on. See if you can introduce them to the joys of being active in environmental improvements, however small. Every little bit counts.
- Try to buy only what you really need and will use a lot, and things that will last (even if their initial cost seems a bit high). William Morris suggested that you should have 'only those things in your house which you know to be useful or believe to be beautiful'.
- Don't try to do it all at once. Take one area where you think you could change to more environmentally friendly approaches and sort that out before trying another area.

We are all bound to pollute the planet to some extent, and we have to live with this. But time is beginning to get short; we cannot allow much more pollution. If we can all try to reduce our own levels of pollution gradually, we shall be making an enormous contribution.

## TAKING ACTION ON ISSUES

The borough or district council and the national government are there to make sure that issues which involve a lot of people, such as schools, traffic, pollution, waste disposal, are looked after. They employ people – teachers, road menders, water inspectors, dustmen – who do the actual work. But it is up to us to tell the council and the government about what we like and do not like, or what might be done differently. One of the best ways of telling them is by writing to them. This does not usually take very long, and keeps them informed of what ordinary people are thinking.

Before you write, find out exactly who you need to write to; for example, if you are worried about litter in your area you need to write to the chairman of the technical services committee of your local council. Decide exactly what you want to say, and try and keep it as short as possible. Make a note of what you said (or keep a copy of your letter), so that you know when you sent it. Councillors are busy people, so although you will get a reply, it may take a little while. If, however, you have not had a reply after about four weeks, you could write again (checking up with your copy to see the date you first wrote and what you said). Make sure you set your letter out clearly, as in the box.

Don't just write if you have a complaint – let them know if there's something you specially like, like this year's flowers at the park or in the high street, or your after-school club. They need to know this as well. And try to get hold of recycled paper to write on; if you keep asking for recycled paper at stationers they might start stocking it.

---

Your name
Your address
Your phone number
Date

Name of person you're writing to
Their address (usually the town hall if it is a councillor)

Dear Councillor _____
Litter (or whatever subject you're writing about)
We have noticed that there seems to be more litter than ever on the Broadway and the streets around. It is becoming very nasty. Would it be possible for the council to provide more bins or to ask the fast food shops to provide them?

Yours sincerely,
(your name)

---

Try to find out who your local councillor is. The library will tell you this, and when and where you can go and meet them. Otherwise, the relevant people you need to know the names of are as follows (their jobs may be slightly differently apportioned depending on your council).

- Leader of the council – leads the majority group. When an issue is urgent it is worth writing to him at the same time as you write to the councillor directly involved.
- Chair of the technical services committee – in charge of cleansing, refuse collection, roads, drains, street lighting.

- Chair of the environmental protection and public health committee – in charge of pollution, health, safety and protection, accident prevention, emergency planning.
- Chair of the community affairs committee – in charge of parks, libraries, arts, entertainments, grants to community organisations.

If you are writing about something and can persuade several other people to write at the same time (but not the same letter), you may make more impact. Even if nothing can be done about what you are concerned with, your letter makes councillors think, and you will at least know why they think nothing can be done. You may have an idea they haven't thought of.

The other person worth writing to is your local member of parliament, who can be written to at the House of Commons, Westminster, London SW1. National figures who share our concerns are the Secretary of State for the Environment, 1 Marsham Street, London SW1, and the Minister of Transport, 2 Marsham Street, London SW1.

Don't forget the local and national newspapers. People do read them and can change their views as a result. And if you don't think all your letter-writing is worth while, it is worth remembering what one MP said, which was that he took letters very seriously because he knew that for each letter that was actually written there were probably another 40 people who felt the same but weren't good at writing.

## ORGANISATIONS FOR CHILDREN, TEENAGERS AND FAMILIES

- *Watch* is a national environment club for children up to 18. Members receive the magazine *Watchword* which briefs them on up-to-date environmental topics while also giving them the chance to take part in national projects. Write to Watch, London Wildlife Trust, 80 York Way, London N1 9AG.
- *Young Ornithologists Club* (YOC), The Lodge, Sandy, Bedfordshire. This is the junior section of the Royal Society for the Protection of Birds. It aims to encourage children to observe and conserve all wildlife, especially birds.
- *Trees for People*, 141 London Road, St. Albans, Hertfordshire AL1 1TA is a voluntary environmental and educational trust whose aims are to encourage young people to

plant, propagate and care for trees and shrubs as a group activity. Trees for People provides seedlings, seed, tools and educational material to schools (and information to anybody who wants it).

- *Streetwork*, c/o Notting Hill Urban Studies Centre, 189 Freston Road, London W10 6TH aims to help people understand issues in the urban environment (within housing, shopping, transport and employment, for example) and helps them to improve their own surroundings.
- *Nature Conservancy Council*, Northminster House, Peterborough PE1 0UH. Responsible to the government for the conservation of fauna and flora and for the selecting, establishing and managing of a series of national nature reserves.
- *Keep Britain Tidy Group*, Bostell House, 27 West Street, Brighton BN1 2RE is a national agency recognised by the Department of the Environment, and it encourages environmental improvement and litter abatement.
- *British Trust for Conservation Volunteers*, 80 York Way, London N1 9AG. Aims to involve people of all ages in practical conservation in town and country. Working holidays are organised at locations all over England, Wales, Scotland and Northern Ireland. In London work goes on all the year round – there are day projects throughout the week and on Sundays and weekend residential projects in the surrounding countryside. You don't have to be a member to come along, and transport, tools, training and experienced guidance are all provided.
- *Earth Action* (Friends of the Earth youth branch, for people from 14–18), c/o Friends of the Earth, 26–28 Underwood Street, London N1 7JQ, 01-490 1555.
- *Youth Hostels Association*, Trevelyan House, 8 St Stephen's Hill, St Albans, Herts AL1 2DY, 0727 55215.
- *The I-Spy Club* publishes a set of informative books which you fill in when you have observed the item described. Very good on nature. When the book is finished, you add up the points you have scored for your observations, send away and get a certificate from David Bellamy, the botanist. Write to the I-Spy Club, 12 Star Road, Partridge Green, Horsham, Sussex RH13 8RA.
- *The Ramblers Association*, 1-5 Wandsworth Road, London SW8 01-582 6826 or 6878. Everything the walker needs to know – including rented cottages, ideas for holidays, equip-

ment. They are also a pressure group and great fighters for
rights of way, etc.

- *National Trust Volunteers* (used to be called the Young
National Trust) are involved in conservation work, mostly at
weekends. The National Trust is responsible for enormous
areas of countryside (stately homes are only a small part of
their work). Some of the volunteer groups include families
with children as young as 10 (accompanied by the parents –
much of the equipment used is dangerous and the NT
organisers cannot be responsible). The National Trust also
run Acorn Camps, which are conservation holidays for
people aged 17 and over. Their address is: Richard Sneyd
(Junior Division), The National Trust, PO Box 12, Westbury
Wiltshire BA13 4NA, 0373 826302. This address and
telephone number are the same for the National Trust
Volunteers.
- *Junior Friends of the Earth*. There is no national organisation, but Friends of the Earth is encouraging the formation
of local groups. They suggest that if you want to start your
own group, write to Muswell Hill JFoE, 2 Elms Avenue,
London N10 2JP, who are co-ordinating local junior groups
and who will provide ideas and information.

## FURTHER READING

### For children
If I were asked to suggest one single book which explained the
global ecological situation for children from 7+, it would be
Usborne's *Ecology – A Practical Introduction With Projects and
Activities.*

Visiting a bookshop with a large children's section (or, better
still, a library) and browsing is a good way to choose books.
However, not only is this not always possible but, because so
many titles are now published, the choice in the shop is necessarily limited to a selection of these titles. Writing or phoning for
publishers' catalogues is quick and easy, and you can browse
through them at home at your leisure. This is well worth doing
as many Green books are not sold through normal outlets and
are better bought by post. If you can't get out to the shops, most
booksellers and many publishers will take a telephone order and
accept payment by credit card, as well as postal payment by
cheque.

It is obviously impossible to list all the publishers and producers of ecologically oriented books, so I have had to select a few, but many others are good too.

- Usborne Publishing, 20 Garrick Street, London WC2 9BJ do excellent information books, most of which contain follow-up activities.
- Ladybird Books, Loughborough, Leicestershire, have many simple explanatory books, good for parents to read with younger children, for less than £1 each.
- A catalogue from Ragged Bears, Ragged Appleshaw, Andover, Hampshire SP11 9HX is a pleasure to read – very tasteful and beautiful books, and not all desperately expensive.
- Exley Publications, 16 Chalk Hill, Watford, Herts WD1 4BN do a limited but excellent list.
- The Rudolf Steiner Press and Mail Order, 38 Museum Street, London WC1A 1LP 01-242 4249 is interesting, although some of the books may seem a bit obscure and esoteric. Many (but not all) of the books they sell are based on Steiner's anthroposophical philosophy but are valuable even if you don't entirely go along with his thinking. They are a million miles from any kind of commercial hype.

The one single book I should like to recommend for children between about 7–13, which deals with the issues of pollution and the future very well, which has a good story line, and has a marvellous child hero who weathers many storms in his battle, almost giving up (and inspiring several children I know to action), is currently out of print – try your library. It is called *Who has poisoned the Sea?* by Audrey Coppard, and was published by Heinemann in 1970. With any luck it might be reissued.

## For adults

This list could go on forever. However, for parental perspective, *The Continuum Concept*, Jean Liedloff, Penguin, London, 1986, is unbeatable.

For a summary of major global problems and where our own action can start, the *Friends of the Earth Handbook*, edited by Jonathon Porritt, Macdonald Optima, London, 1987, is a good basic text, whether or not you are a Friend of the Earth.

The book that woke much of the world up to the problem of

chemical pollution was *Silent Spring*, Rachel Carson, Pelican, London, 1962, but still in print. She is a scientist but writes like a poet, and explains how the indiscriminate use of chemicals will eventually kill humanity – and how we could avert this end.

*The Turning Point*, Fritjof Capra, Flamingo, London, 1983 is a big book by a physicist, in which he puts forward the case for discarding our old mechanistic scientific attitudes in favour of a holistic approach to world problems. Comprehensive and transformational.

*Tools for Conviviality*, Ivan Illich, Calder & Boyars, London, 1973 is a critique of industrial society. If you need convincing that man is now serving his machines rather than vice versa, try this book, which does it in about 100 pages.

*How to be Green*, John Button, Century Hutchinson, London, 1989. Catalogue of all the ways in which you can make your everyday life more eco-friendly. Very easy to use – topic headings, what you can do, what needs to change. Very useful for the person wishing to make gradual changes, as it is so neatly compartmentalized.

On a more practical note, sorting one's own life out, which is where it all starts, needs a certain amount of information and help. As well as *Home Ecology* (Karen Christensen, Arlington, London, 1989), see *The Green Consumer Guide* (John Elkington and Julia Hailes, Gollancz, London, 1988) and *Green Pages* (compiled by John Button, Macdonald Optima, London, 1988).

It might be worth getting in touch with LifeStyle, which concerns itself with the problems, rewards and practicalities of leading a simpler life. LifeStyle coined the phrase 'Live simply that others may simply live.' The Secretary is Mrs Margaret Smith, Manor Farm, Little Gidding, Cambs PE17 5RJ.

# 14.
# TOWARDS A SUSTAINABLE FUTURE

Waving banners and running campaigns are necessary steps in the raising of public consciousness. But the results of such campaigns in getting specific environmental malpractices reduced are no more than temporary successes unless they become the beginning of a major shift in attitudes.

The present generation of parents has been brought up within the tradition of economic growth outlined in Chapter 1, which has taught us to value the masculine elements of life (rational, demanding, competitive, aggressive, analytic) more highly than the feminine (intuitive, cooperative, responsive, synthesising). The terms masculine and feminine do not imply that members of each sex possess these characteristics; in many ways, the terminology is unfortunate. The Chinese talk about yin and yang, which is what is meant in the present context. Both elements are necessary in individuals and in the world for life to be balanced. However, in view of the historical imbalance in favour of the masculine characteristics, particularly in the last 250 years, accelerated by the onset of industrialisation, the feminine elements need to be powerfully reasserted in order that the balance be redressed.

The masculine, industrial imperative, as we have seen, has extended its tentacles through the whole of life so that it is now controlling us from within our homes and families. We need to free ourselves and our children from its power, for we cannot hope to correct global damage unless we can find a non-destructive lifestyle that gives us and our children inner satisfaction and joy. If enough people can do so, the need for growth economics and for man's enslavement to the machine will begin to diminish and we will be free to pursue other, more humane and less damaging, purposes in life. It is no sacrifice. To substitute joy, responsibility for oneself and others, optimism and worthwhile activity for grim determination, self-aggrandisement, acquisition and overwork is to gain. But it cannot all be done in one go. Relinquishing long-held values is not an easy job, particularly when conformist, materialist values can make us feel guilty and publicly undervalued when we step out of line. But more and more people are discovering the delights of a Greener life and the rewards of fulfilling their own truly creative potential. How each family goes about it is a matter of individual choice. What I have attempted to do is to throw up ideas which people have found useful. Others may totally disagree with them and be trying out different ideas (hopefully). There are many ways to similar solutions.

Nurture and care remain at the heart of the matter. These are mostly, but not entirely, feminine characteristics. If you don't believe how far society has downgraded these essential elements, a glance at pay scales provides ample evidence. Nurses and sweepers of streets are paid vastly less than senior managers of firms producing unduly large numbers of outrageously luxurious metal machines to clutter up roads, kill people, destroy the atmosphere and over-accelerate the pace of life. The manufacture of these monsters is described as 'productive', despite the fact that they destroy as much as they create, while attention to the physical and mental health of human beings, or the maintenance of a pleasant environment, is not considered productive.

The way that we as carers can assert ourselves is to reject, as far as each of us is able, the values and products of the destroyers. This takes great confidence, and is a gradual process. But those who decide to do so will find they are in good company. We also need to speak out. Wherever there is an opportunity to write to a firm or a politician, or to speak to them, we must make an effort to ensure that our voices are heard. Children can do this too. For the Green, there is time. The average Briton spends, on average, three hours a day shopping and three hours a day watching television. We have only to do a little less of both to have the time to write a letter. Green attitudes and the Green movement are growing organically; and if Greens could make their care, optimism, energy and thrift fashionable, and second nature to their children, the future of humanity could be saved and the pointlessness of much of our stressful, dehumanised, alienated existence be replaced by a sense of inspiring purpose.

'Good morning', said the little prince.
'Good morning', said the railway switchman.
'What do you do here?' the little prince asked.
'I sort out travellers, in bundles of a thousand', said the switchman. 'I send off the trains that carry them; now to the right, now to the left.' And a brilliantly lighted express train shook the switchman's cabin as it rushed by with a roar like thunder.
'They are in a great hurry', said the little prince. 'What are they looking for?'
'Not even the locomotive engineer knows that', said the switchman.
And a second brilliantly lighted express thundered by, in the opposite direction.
'Are they coming back already?' demanded the little prince.
'These are not the same ones', said the switchman.
'It is an exchange.'
'Were they not satisfied where they were?' asked the little prince.
'No one is ever satisfied where he is', said the switchman.
And they heard the roaring thunder of a third brilliantly lighted express.
'Are they pursuing the first travellers?' demanded the little prince.
'They are pursuing nothing at all', said the switchman. 'They are asleep in there, or if they are not asleep they are yawning. Only the children are flattening their noses against the window-panes.'
'Only the children know what they are looking for', said the little prince. 'They waste their time over a rag doll and it becomes very important to them; and if anybody takes it away from them, they cry ...'
'They are lucky', the switchman said.

*The Little Prince*, Antoine de Saint-Exupéry

# INDEX

stimulation, 38, 150
summer festivals, 134

technologies, appropriate, 16–19
technologies, intermediate,
    18–19
technology, 111–12
teenagers, 157–67
teenagers, organisations for,
    195–97
television, 67–68, 125, 126, 129,
    148, 150–51
temperature, 45–46
*Times Educational Supplement*,
    108
toddlers, 58–71
toys, 31–36, 91–93, 102, 128
tranquillisers, 3
trees, 179–80
trolley, 36, *37*

tumble-driers, 78
Tweedie, Jill, 27

VDU screens, 111

walking, 67
walks, 121
washing, 27–28
Watch, 141
Whitsun, 134
*The Whole Health Manual*, 50
Winn, Mary, 142
winter festivals, 136–37
Woodcraft Folk, 129, 141
Woods, Dr David, 112
working parents, 70, 123
World Health Organisation, 43

youth hostelling, 165

# Green books from Optima ...

## FRIENDS OF THE EARTH HANDBOOK
### Edited by Jonathon Porritt
'. . . compiled by the staff and supporters of Friends of the Earth
and contains all the practical advice you need to become a good
environmentalist.'                                  *The Guardian*
£5.99                              Printed on recycled paper


## GREEN PAGES
### A Directory of Natural Products, Services, Resources and Ideas
### Compiled by John Button
'. . . an absolute must for the all-round green consumer.'
                                                    *Nineteen*
£11.99                             Printed on recycled paper


## A GREEN MANIFESTO
### Policies For A Green Future
### Sandy Irvine and Alec Ponton
'. . . not just another book about the state of the environment . . .
a hard-headed presentation of radical alternatives, based on a
fundamental reinterpretation of the relationship between
humankind and planet Earth.'                 *Jonathon Porritt*
£6.99

## THE FUTURE IS NOW
### Deirdre Rhys-Thomas
Leading personalities from public affairs, the media, science
and the health professions voice their concerns about the
environmental dangers facing the planet.
£4.99                                    Printed on recycled paper


## DOWN THE DRAIN
### Water, Pollution and Privatisation
### Stuart Gordon
A searching – and disturbing – investigation of the use and
abuse of our most valuable natural resource – water.
£5.99


## GUIDE TO GAIA
### Michael Allaby
An introduction to the Gaia hypothesis, and the way it can be
used to look at environmental problems.
£6.99

All Optima books are available at your bookshop or newsagent, or can be ordered from the following address:

Optima, Cash Sales Department,
PO Box 11, Falmouth, Cornwall TR10 9EN

Please send cheque or postal order (no currency), and allow 60p for postage and packing for the first book, plus 25p for the second book and 15p for each additional book ordered up to a maximum charge of £1.90 in the UK.

Customers in Eire and BFPO please allow 60p for the first book, 25p for the second book plus 15p per copy for the next 7 books, thereafter 9p per book.

Overseas customers please allow £1.25 for postage and packing for the first books and 28p per copy for each additional book.